The Weekend Fisherman's Cookbook

Jordan Rivers

Published by A. I. Rivers, 2024.

While every precaution has been taken in the preparation of this book, the publisher assumes no responsibility for errors or omissions, or for damages resulting from the use of the information contained herein.

THE WEEKEND FISHERMAN'S COOKBOOK

First edition. April 14, 2024.

Copyright © 2024 Jordan Rivers.

ISBN: 979-8224189656

Written by Jordan Rivers.

Table of Contents

This book is dedicated to my brother Doug who puts the
MAN in Fisherman!

<u>Chapter1: Equipment and Preparation</u>

Essential fishing equipment and tips for a successful fishing trip.

Cleaning and filleting techniques to ensure your fish is ready for cooking.

Cleaning and filleting fish properly is essential to ensure that they are ready for cooking. Here's a step-by-step guide to help you clean and fillet your catch effectively:

1. <u>Gather the necessary equipment</u>:

A sturdy cutting board

A sharp fillet knife

A bucket or container for discarding waste

2. <u>Prepare a clean and well-lit area</u>:

Ensure that your workspace is clean and free of any potential contaminants.

A well-lit area will help you see what you are doing clearly.

3. <u>Scaling the fish (if necessary)</u>:

If your fish has scales, use the backside of the knife or a scaling tool to remove them.

Start at the tail and move towards the head, using short, firm strokes. Rinse the fish to remove any loose scales.

4. <u>Gutting the fish</u>:

Locate the anus of the fish, usually located near the vent.

Make a shallow incision around the anus using the tip of the knife.

Extend the incision up towards the head, careful not to puncture the internal organs.

Reach inside the cavity and remove the internal organs, including the liver, intestines, and gills.

5. <u>Rinsing the fish</u>:

Rinse the fish thoroughly, both inside and out, under cold running water to remove any remaining blood, slime, or internal debris.

6. <u>Filleting the fish</u>:

Lay the fish on its side and make a small incision behind the gills, just above the pectoral fin.

Run the knife along the backbone, making long, smooth strokes towards the tail.

Use your non-dominant hand to hold the fish firmly while filleting.

Repeat the process on the other side to obtain two fillets.

7. <u>Removing the rib bones</u>:

Lay a fillet with the skin side down on the cutting board.

Locate the rib bones and make a cut just above them, being careful not to cut through the skin.

Use a gentle sawing motion with the knife to separate the fillet from the rib bones.

8. <u>Trimming and skinning (optional)</u>:

Trim any excess fat or dark meat from the fillets, if desired.

To remove the skin, hold the tail end of the fillet firmly and insert the knife between the skin and flesh.

Using a sawing motion, slide the knife along the fillet while holding onto the skin, separating it from the flesh.

9. <u>Rinse and store</u>:

Rinse the fillets again under cold water to remove any stray scales or debris.

Pat the fillets dry with a clean paper towel before storing them properly, either by refrigerating or freezing them.

Remember, practice makes perfect, and it's important to be cautious and take your time while cleaning and filleting fish. Soon enough, you'll become more proficient and efficient in preparing your fish for a delicious meal!

Chapter 2: Appetizers and Small Bites

Crispy Fish Fritters with Spicy Remoulade Sauce
Fish Fritters with Spicy Remoulade Sauce Recipe:
Ingredients:
1 pound of boneless, skinless fish fillets (such as walleye, perch, or catfish)
1/2 cup all-purpose flour
1/4 cup cornmeal
1/2 teaspoon baking powder
1/2 teaspoon paprika
1/2 teaspoon garlic powder
1/4 teaspoon cayenne pepper (adjust to taste)
1/4 teaspoon salt
1/4 teaspoon black pepper
1/2 cup buttermilk
1 large egg, beaten
Vegetable oil, for frying
Spicy Remoulade Sauce:
1/2 cup mayonnaise
2 tablespoons Dijon mustard
1 tablespoon pickle relish
1 tablespoon hot sauce (adjust to taste)
1 tablespoon lemon juice
1 green onion, finely chopped
1 tablespoon chopped fresh parsley
Salt and pepper, to taste

<u>Instructions</u>:

1. Cut the fish fillets into small bite-sized pieces and set aside.

2. In a shallow dish, whisk together the flour, cornmeal, baking powder, paprika, garlic powder, cayenne pepper, salt, and black pepper.

3. In a separate bowl, combine the buttermilk and beaten egg.

4. Dip the fish pieces into the buttermilk mixture, allowing any excess to drip off, and then coat them in the flour mixture. Shake off the excess flour coating.

5. Heat vegetable oil in a deep frying pan or Dutch oven over medium-high heat until it reaches a temperature of 350°F (175°C).

6. Fry the fish fritters in batches, turning occasionally, until golden brown and crispy, which should take about 3-4 minutes per batch. Avoid overcrowding the pan to ensure even cooking.

7. Using a slotted spoon or tongs, transfer the cooked fritters to a paper towel-lined plate to drain any excess oil.

8. For the Spicy Remoulade Sauce, in a small bowl, whisk together the mayonnaise, Dijon mustard, pickle relish, hot sauce, lemon juice, green onion, and chopped parsley. Season with salt and pepper to taste.

9. Serve the fish fritters hot, along with the Spicy Remoulade Sauce for dipping.

Enjoy your delicious fish fritters with a spicy kick of Remoulade Sauce! These crispy bites make for a delightful appetizer or even a main course when paired with a side salad or coleslaw.

<u>Smoked Trout Spread on Crostini Recipe</u>:

<u>Ingredients</u>:

8 ounces smoked trout fillets; skin removed

4 ounces cream cheese, softened

2 tablespoons mayonnaise

1 tablespoon lemon juice

1 tablespoon chopped fresh dill

1 tablespoon chopped fresh chives

Salt and black pepper, to taste

Baguette or French bread, sliced into thin rounds (crostini)

Olive oil, for brushing

<u>Instructions:</u>

1. In a medium bowl, flake the smoked trout fillets into small pieces using a fork.

2. Add the cream cheese, mayonnaise, lemon juice, chopped dill, and chopped chives to the bowl with the smoked trout.

3. Season the mixture with a pinch of salt and black pepper, then stir well until all the ingredients are thoroughly combined.

4. Preheat the oven to 350°F (175°C).

5. Arrange the baguette or French bread slices on a baking sheet. Lightly brush both sides of the slices with olive oil.

6. Toast the bread slices in the preheated oven for about 8-10 minutes, or until they turn golden and crispy. Remove from the oven and let them cool slightly.

7. Once the crostini are cooled, spread a generous amount of the smoked trout mixture onto each slice.

8. Optionally, garnish the crostini with additional chopped dill or chives.

9. Serve the smoked trout spread on crostini as an appetizer or as part of a charcuterie board.

The creamy and smoky flavors of the smoked trout spread paired with the crispy crostini make for a fantastic party or gathering snack. Enjoy!

<u>Grilled Perch skewers with Lemon Dill Sauce</u>

Grilled Perch skewers with Lemon Dill Sauce sounds delicious! Here's a recipe to help you make it:

<u>Ingredients:</u>

1 pound Perch fillets, cut into chunks

Wooden skewers (soaked in water for 30 minutes to prevent burning)

1 lemon, juiced

2 tablespoons olive oil

1 tablespoon chopped fresh dill

Salt and pepper to taste

For the Lemon Dill Sauce:

1/2 cup mayonnaise

2 tablespoons lemon juice

1 tablespoon chopped fresh dill

1 clove garlic, minced

Salt and pepper to taste

Instructions:

1. Preheat your grill to medium high heat.

2. In a bowl, combine the lemon juice, olive oil, chopped dill, salt, and pepper. Toss the Perch chunks in this marinade and let them sit for about15 minutes.

3. While the fish is marinating, prepare the Lemon Dill Sauce. In a separate bowl, combine the mayonnaise, lemon juice, chopped dill, minced garlic, salt, and pepper. Mix everything together until well combined. Taste and adjust the seasonings as needed.

4. Thread the marinated Perch chunks onto the soaked wooden skewers. Make sure to leave a little space between each piece to allow for even cooking.

5. Place the skewers on the preheated grill and cook for about 34 minutes per side, or until the fish is cooked through and opaque.

6. Remove the skewers from the grill and serve them hot with the Lemon Dill Sauce on the side.

Enjoy your delicious grilled Perch skewers with the zesty Lemon Dill Sauce! It makes for a flavorful and refreshing meal.

Chapter 3: Soups and Chowders

Creamy Salmon Chowder with Dill

Creamy Salmon Chowder with dill is a comforting and flavorful dish. Here's a recipe to guide you through the process:

Ingredients:

1 pound salmon fillet, skin removed and cut into bite sized pieces

4 slices bacon, chopped

1 medium onion, diced

2 cloves garlic, minced

2 medium potatoes, peeled and diced

2 cups chicken or vegetable broth

1 cup heavy cream

1 cup whole milk

1 tablespoon all-purpose flour

2 tablespoons fresh dill, chopped

Salt and pepper to taste

Instructions:

1. In a large pot or Dutch oven, cook the chopped bacon over medium heat until crispy. Remove the bacon from the pot using a slotted spoon and set it aside, leaving the bacon drippings in the pot.

2. Add the diced onion to the pot and cook until softened and translucent, about 5 minutes. Stir in the minced garlic and cook for an additional minute.

3. Add the diced potatoes and chicken or vegetable broth to the pot. Bring the mixture to a boil, then reduce the heat, and let it simmer until the potatoes are tender, about 10-15 minutes.

4. In a separate bowl, whisk together the heavy cream, milk, and all-purpose flour until well combined. Pour this mixture into the pot with the potatoes and broth, stirring well.

5. Add the salmon pieces to the pot and gently simmer until the salmon is cooked through and flakes easily with a fork, about 5-7 minutes. Be careful not to overcook the fish.

6. Stir in the chopped dill and season the chowder with salt and pepper to taste. Let it simmer for an additional 2-3 minutes to allow the flavors to meld together.

7. Serve the creamy salmon chowder hot, garnished with the crispy bacon bits on top. You can also sprinkle some additional fresh dill for extra flavor.

Enjoy your creamy Salmon Chowder with dill! It's a hearty and delicious soup that is perfect for chilly days.

<u>Fisherman's Stew with Whitefish and Vegetables</u>

Fisherman's stew with whitefish and vegetables is a hearty and flavorful dish. Here's a recipe to help you make it:

<u>Ingredients</u>:

1 pound whitefish fillets, cut into chunks

2 tablespoons olive oil

1 onion, chopped

2 cloves garlic, minced

1 red bell pepper, chopped

1 carrot, peeled and sliced

1 zucchini, sliced

1 can diced tomatoes (14 ounces)

3 cups fish or vegetable broth

1 teaspoon dried thyme

1 teaspoon dried oregano

Salt and pepper to taste

Fresh parsley, chopped (for garnish)

<u>Instructions</u>:

1. Heat olive oil in a large pot or Dutch oven over medium heat. Add the chopped onion and minced garlic and cook until the onion becomes translucent and fragrant.

2. Add the red bell pepper, carrot, and zucchini to the pot. Sauté the vegetables for about 5 minutes, or until they start to soften.

3. Pour in the diced tomatoes (including the juice) and fish or vegetable broth. Add the dried thyme, dried oregano, salt, and pepper. Stir everything together.

4. Bring the stew to a simmer and let it cook for about 10 minutes, allowing the flavors to meld together.

5. Gently add the whitefish chunks to the pot and cook until they are opaque and cooked through, about 5-7 minutes. Be careful not to overcook the fish.

6. Taste the stew and adjust the seasonings if needed. You can add more salt, pepper, or herbs according to your preference.

7. Serve the Fisherman's stew hot, garnished with freshly chopped parsley. It pairs well with crusty bread, which can be used to soak up the flavorful broth.

Enjoy your delicious Fisherman's stew with whitefish and vegetables! It's a comforting and satisfying meal that is perfect for seafood lovers.

Spicy Tomato Bisque with Catfish

Spicy Tomato Bisque with Catfish sounds like a delicious combination! Here's a recipe to help you make it:

Ingredients:

1 pound catfish fillets, cut into chunks

2 tablespoons olive oil

1 onion, chopped

2 cloves garlic, minced

1 jalapeño pepper, seeded and minced

1 red bell pepper, chopped

1 can diced tomatoes (14 ounces)

2 cups vegetable or fish broth

1 cup heavy cream

1 teaspoon paprika

1/2 teaspoon cayenne pepper

Salt and pepper to taste

Fresh cilantro, chopped (for garnish)

<u>Instructions</u>:

1. Heat olive oil in a large pot or Dutch oven over medium heat. Add the chopped onion, minced garlic, and minced jalapeño pepper. Cook until the onion becomes translucent, and the peppers are slightly softened.

2. Add the red bell pepper to the pot and cook for an additional 2-3 minutes.

3. Pour in the diced tomatoes (including the juice) and vegetable or fish broth. Stir in the paprika, cayenne pepper, salt, and pepper. Bring the mixture to a simmer and let it cook for about 10 minutes, allowing the flavors to meld together.

4. Use an immersion blender or transfer the mixture to a blender to puree until smooth. Be careful when blending hot liquids. If using a blender, blend in batches and return the soup to the pot.

5. Add the catfish chunks to the pot and simmer for about 5-7 minutes, or until the fish is cooked through and flakes easily with a fork.

6. Stir in the heavy cream and let the soup simmer for an additional 2-3 minutes to heat through.

7. Taste the bisque and adjust the seasonings if needed. Add more salt, pepper, paprika, or cayenne pepper according to your preference.

8. Serve the spicy tomato bisque hot, garnished with freshly chopped cilantro. Enjoy it as a comforting and flavorful soup!

Note: If you prefer a milder version, you can adjust the amount of jalapeño pepper and cayenne pepper to suit your taste.

I hope you enjoy making and savoring this Spicy Tomato Bisque with Catfish!

Chapter 4: Grilling and Roasting

Grilled Rainbow Trout with Herbed Butter

Grilling Rainbow trout with Herbed butter is a great way to enhance its natural flavors. Here's a recipe for grilled Rainbow trout with Herbed butter:

Ingredients:

2 Rainbow trout fillets

4 tablespoons unsalted butter, softened

2 tablespoons fresh parsley, finely chopped

2 tablespoons fresh chives, finely chopped

1 tablespoon fresh lemon juice

1 clove garlic, minced

Salt and pepper to taste

Lemon wedges (for serving)

Instructions:

1. Preheat your grill to medium-high heat.

2. In a small bowl, combine the softened butter, chopped parsley, chopped chives, minced garlic, fresh lemon juice, salt, and pepper. Mix everything together until well combined, creating the herbed butter.

3. Pat the Rainbow trout fillets dry with a paper towel. Season them with salt and pepper on both sides.

4. Spread a generous amount of herbed butter on the flesh side of each fillet.

5. Place the fillets, skin side down, on the preheated grill. Close the lid and grill for about 4-6 minutes per side, or until the fish is cooked through and flakes easily with a fork.

6. Carefully remove the grilled Rainbow trout fillets from the grill and transfer them to a serving plate.

7. Serve the Rainbow trout hot, garnished with additional fresh herbs if desired. Squeeze some fresh lemon juice over the fillets before eating.

Grilled Rainbow trout with Herbed butter is a delightful and flavorful dish that pairs well with steamed vegetables, rice, or a fresh salad. Enjoy your meal!

Seared Lake Bass with Citrus Glaze

To make Seared Lake Bass with Citrus glaze, follow this recipe:

Ingredients:

2 Lake Bass fillets

1 tablespoon olive oil

Salt and pepper to taste

For the Citrus Glaze:

¼ cup orange juice

1 tablespoon lime juice

1 tablespoon honey

½ teaspoon grated orange zest

½ teaspoon grated lime zest

Instructions:

1. In a small bowl, whisk together the orange juice, lime juice, honey, orange zest, and lime zest. Set the citrus glaze aside.

2. Pat the Lake Bass fillets dry with a paper towel. Season them with salt and pepper on both sides.

3. Heat olive oil in a skillet over medium-high heat. Once the oil is hot, add the seasoned Lake Bass fillets, skin side down.

4. Sear the fillets for about 3-4 minutes on each side, or until the fish is cooked through and develops a golden-brown crust. The cooking time may vary depending on the thickness of the fillets. Ensure the fish is cooked to an internal temperature of145°F (63°C).

5. Remove the seared Lake Bass fillets from the skillet and transfer them to a serving plate. Allow the fish to rest for a minute.

6. Drizzle the prepared citrus glaze over the seared fillets. You can reserve some glaze for serving, if desired.

Serve the Seared Lake Bass with Citrus glaze immediately while still hot. It pairs well with a side of steamed vegetables or rice. Enjoy your meal!

<u>Whole Grilled Pike Stuffed with Fresh Herbs</u>

To make a whole grilled Pike stuffed with fresh herbs, follow these steps:

<u>Ingredients</u>:

1 whole Pike (cleaned and gutted)

Assorted fresh herbs (such as parsley, dill, thyme, and rosemary)

Lemon slices

Olive oil

Salt and pepper to taste

<u>Instructions</u>:

1. Preheat your grill to medium-high heat.

2. Prepare the Pike by rinsing it under cold water and patting it dry with a paper towel. Season the inside and outside of the fish generously with salt and pepper.

3. Stuff the cavity of the Pike with a generous amount of fresh herbs, filling it up fully. You can use a combination of parsley, dill, thyme, and rosemary. The herbs will infuse the fish with aromatic flavors as it grills.

4. Place a few slices of lemon on top of the herbs inside the Pike's cavity. This will add a bright citrus flavor to the fish.

5. Brush the outer skin of the Pike with olive oil to prevent sticking and provide moisture.

6. Place the whole stuffed Pike directly on the preheated grill. Close the lid and cook for about 15-20 minutes per side, or until the fish is

cooked through and flakes easily when tested with a fork. The cooking time may vary depending on the size of the fish.

7. Carefully flip the Pike halfway through the cooking process to ensure even grilling on both sides.

8. Once the fish is cooked, remove it from the grill and transfer it to a serving platter.

9. Serve the whole grilled Pike hot, allowing your guests to enjoy the flavorful combination of the tender fish and the infusion of fresh herbs. You can garnish with additional fresh herbs and lemon slices if desired.

Grilling a whole Pike stuffed with fresh herbs is a delicious and impressive way to enjoy this fish. It's perfect for sharing at a gathering or special dinner.

Chapter 5: Pan-Fried Delights

Pan-Fried Walleye with Lemon-Caper Sauce

To make pan-fried Walleye with lemon caper sauce, you can follow these instructions:

Ingredients:

2 Walleye fillets

1/4 cup all-purpose flour

Salt and pepper to taste

Olive oil for frying

For the Lemon Caper Sauce:

2 tablespoons butter

2 tablespoons fresh lemon juice

1 tablespoon capers

1 tablespoon chopped fresh parsley

Salt and pepper to taste

Instructions:

1. Rinse the Walleye fillets under cold water and pat them dry with a paper towel. Season both sides of the fillets with salt and pepper.

2. Place the all-purpose flour on a plate and dredge the fillets in the flour, making sure to coat them evenly.

3. Heat a couple of tablespoons of olive oil in a skillet over medium-high heat.

4. Once the oil is hot, carefully place the floured Walleye fillets in the skillet. Cook for about 3-4 minutes on each side, or until the fish is golden brown and cooked through. The cooking time may vary

depending on the thickness of the fillets. Ensure the fish is cooked to an internal temperature of 145°F (63°C).

5. While the fish is cooking, prepare the lemon caper sauce. In a small saucepan, melt the butter over low heat. Add the lemon juice, capers, chopped parsley, salt, and pepper. Stir everything together and let it simmer for a minute or two until the flavors combine.

6. Once the Walleye fillets are cooked, transfer them to a serving plate. Drizzle the lemon caper sauce over the fillets, ensuring it covers them evenly. You can also spoon some extra capers and chopped parsley on top for added flavor and presentation.

Serve the pan-fried Walleye with lemon caper sauce immediately while still hot. This dish pairs well with steamed vegetables or a side of rice pilaf. Enjoy your meal!

Crispy Skin-On Crappie with Garlic Butter

To make Crispy skin-on Crappie with garlic butter, follow these steps:

Ingredients:

4 Crappie fillets, skin on

2 tablespoons butter

2 cloves garlic, minced

Salt and pepper to taste

Olive oil for frying

Instructions:

1. Rinse the Crappie fillets under cold water and pat them dry with a paper towel. Season both sides of the fillets with salt and pepper.

2. Heat a couple of tablespoons of olive oil in a skillet over medium-high heat.

3. Once the oil is hot, carefully place the Crappie fillets in the skillet, skin side down. Cook for about 3-4 minutes on each side, or until the skin becomes crispy and the fish is cooked through. The cooking time may vary depending on the thickness of the fillets. Ensure the fish is cooked to an internal temperature of 145°F (63°C).

4. While the fish is cooking, melt the butter in a small saucepan over low heat. Once melted, add the minced garlic, and cook for a minute or two until fragrant. Be careful not to burn the garlic.

5. Once the Crappie fillets are cooked, transfer them to a serving plate. Drizzle the garlic butter over the fillets, ensuring it covers them evenly. You can also sprinkle some freshly chopped parsley on top for added flavor and presentation.

Serve the Crispy skin-on Crappie with garlic butter immediately while still hot. It pairs well with a side of roasted vegetables or a fresh salad. Enjoy your meal!

<u>Cajun-Style Catfish Nuggets with Remoulade Sauce</u>

To make Cajun-style catfish nuggets with Remoulade sauce, follow these instructions:

<u>Ingredients for Catfish Nuggets</u>:

1 pound catfish fillets, cut into bite sized nuggets

1 cup buttermilk

1 cup all-purpose flour

2 tablespoons Cajun seasoning

1 teaspoon paprika

1/2 teaspoon garlic powder

1/2 teaspoon onion powder

Vegetable oil for frying

Salt and pepper to taste

<u>Ingredients for Remoulade Sauce</u>:

1/2 cup mayonnaise

2 tablespoons Dijon mustard

1 tablespoon pickle relish

1 tablespoon fresh lemon juice

1 tablespoon chopped fresh parsley

2 teaspoons Cajun seasoning

1 teaspoon hot sauce (optional)

<u>Instructions</u>:

1. Place the catfish nuggets in a shallow dish and pour the buttermilk over them. Let the nuggets soak in the buttermilk for 15-20 minutes. The buttermilk helps tenderize the fish and adds flavor.

2. In a separate bowl, combine the all-purpose flour, Cajun seasoning, paprika, garlic powder, onion powder, salt, and pepper. Mix the dry ingredients together until well combined.

3. Heat vegetable oil in a deep skillet or Dutch oven over medium-high heat. The oil should be about 1 inch deep.

4. Remove the catfish nuggets from the buttermilk, allowing any excess buttermilk to drip off. Dredge each nugget in the seasoned flour mixture, coating them evenly.

5. Carefully drop the coated catfish nuggets into the hot oil, a few at a time, without overcrowding the pan. Fry them for about 3-4 minutes per side or until they turn golden brown and crispy. Make sure to cook them in batches, if necessary.

6. Once the catfish nuggets are cooked, use a slotted spoon or tongs to remove them from the oil and transfer them to a plate lined with paper towels. This will help absorb any excess oil.

7. While the catfish nuggets are resting, prepare the Remoulade sauce. In a small bowl, combine the mayonnaise, Dijon mustard, pickle relish, fresh lemon juice, chopped parsley, Cajun seasoning, and hot sauce (if using). Stir everything together until well combined.

8. Serve the Cajun-style catfish nuggets hot, with the Remoulade sauce on the side for dipping. The spicy and tangy Remoulade sauce pairs perfectly with the crispy catfish nuggets.

Enjoy your Cajun-style catfish nuggets with Remoulade sauce! It's a flavorful and satisfying dish that's sure to impress.

Chapter 6: Baked and Broiled Goodness

Oven-Baked Lake Trout with Parmesan Crust

To make oven-baked lake trout with a Parmesan crust, follow these steps:

Ingredients:

4 lake trout fillets

1 cup Panko breadcrumbs

1/2 cup grated Parmesan cheese

1/4 cup fresh parsley, finely chopped

2 tablespoons melted butter

1 tablespoon lemon zest

1/2 teaspoon garlic powder

Salt and pepper to taste

Lemon wedges (for serving)

Instructions:

1. Preheat your oven to 425°F (220°C). Line a baking sheet with parchment paper or lightly grease it.

2. In a mixing bowl, combine the Panko breadcrumbs, grated Parmesan cheese, chopped parsley, melted butter, lemon zest, garlic powder, salt, and pepper. Mix everything together until well combined. This will be the Parmesan crust for your lake trout.

3. Place the lake trout fillets on the prepared baking sheet. If the fillets have skin on, place them skin-side down.

4. Divide the Parmesan crust mixture evenly among the fillets, pressing it onto the top surface of each fillet to form a nice crust.

5. Bake the lake trout in the preheated oven for about12-15 minutes, or until the fish is cooked through and the crust turns golden brown and crispy. The cooking time may vary depending on the thickness of the fillets. Ensure the fish is cooked to an internal temperature of145°F (63°C).

6. Once the lake trout is cooked, remove it from the oven and let it rest for a few minutes.

7. Serve the oven-baked lake trout hot, garnished with additional chopped parsley and lemon wedges for squeezing over the fish. The Parmesan crust adds a delightful, savory flavor and texture to the tender trout.

This oven-baked lake trout with a Parmesan crust is a delightful and satisfying dish, perfect for a flavorful dinner. Enjoy!

Broiled Bluegill Fillets with Herb Crumbs

To make broiled bluegill fillets with herb crumbs, follow these steps:

Ingredients:

4 bluegill fillets

1 cup breadcrumbs (preferably Panko)

2 tablespoons grated Parmesan cheese

2 tablespoons chopped fresh herbs (such as parsley, thyme, and chives)

2 tablespoons melted butter

1 tablespoon lemon zest

Salt and pepper to taste

Lemon wedges (for serving)

Instructions:

1. Preheat your broiler to high heat.

2. In a mixing bowl, combine the breadcrumbs, grated Parmesan cheese, chopped fresh herbs, melted butter, lemon zest, salt, and pepper. Mix everything together until well combined. This will be the herb crumb mixture to top your bluegill fillets.

3. Place the bluegill fillets on a broiler pan or a baking sheet lined with aluminum foil for easy cleanup.

4. Sprinkle the herb crumb mixture evenly over the top of each bluegill fillet, pressing it lightly to adhere.

5. Place the pan with the fillets under the preheated broiler, about 4-6 inches away from the heat source. Broil for about 5-7 minutes, or until the crumbs are golden brown and the fish is cooked through. The cooking time may vary depending on the thickness of the fillets. Ensure the fish is cooked to an internal temperature of145°F (63°C).

6. Keep a close eye on the fillets while broiling to prevent them from burning. If the crumbs start to brown too quickly, you can lightly tent the fillets with aluminum foil.

7. Once the bluegill fillets are cooked and the crumb topping is crispy, remove them from the broiler.

8. Serve the broiled bluegill fillets hot, garnished with additional chopped fresh herbs and lemon wedges for squeezing over the fish. The herb crumbs add a delightful crunch and flavor to the tender bluegill fillets.

Enjoy your broiled bluegill fillets with herb crumbs! It's a delicious way to highlight the delicate flavors of the fish.

Stuffed Salmon Roll-Ups with Creamy Spinach

To make stuffed Salmon roll-ups with creamy spinach, follow these steps:

Ingredients:

4 Salmon fillets, skin-off

2 cups fresh spinach, chopped

1/2 cup cream cheese

1/4 cup grated Parmesan cheese

2 cloves garlic, minced

1 tablespoon olive oil

Salt and pepper to taste

Toothpicks or kitchen twine

<u>Instructions</u>:

1. Preheat your oven to 375°F (190°C).

2. In a skillet, heat the olive oil over medium heat. Add the minced garlic and sauté for about 1-2 minutes until fragrant.

3. Add the chopped spinach to the skillet and cook until wilted, stirring occasionally. This should take about 3-4 minutes. Remove the skillet from heat.

4. In a mixing bowl, combine the wilted spinach, cream cheese, grated Parmesan cheese, salt, and pepper. Stir everything together until well mixed and the cheese has melted.

5. Lay the Salmon fillets flat on a clean surface. Divide the spinach mixture equally among the fillets, spreading it evenly over the surface.

6. Starting from one end, carefully roll up each Salmon fillet. Secure the rolls with toothpicks or tie them with kitchen twine to keep them closed. Make sure to remove the toothpicks or twine before serving.

7. Place the stuffed Salmon roll-ups in a baking dish, seam side down, and transfer them to the preheated oven.

8. Bake the Salmon roll-ups for approximately 15-20 minutes, or until the fish is cooked through and flakes easily with a fork. The cooking time may vary depending on the thickness of the fillets.

9. Once the Salmon roll-ups are cooked, remove them from the oven and let them rest for a few minutes.

10. Serve the stuffed Salmon roll-ups with creamy spinach hot, garnished with additional grated Parmesan cheese and a side of your choice, such as roasted vegetables or mashed potatoes.

Enjoy your delicious stuffed Salmon roll-ups with creamy spinach! It's a beautiful, flavorful dish that combines savory Salmon with creamy spinach filling.

Chapter 7: Healthy and Light Options

Steamed Tilapia with Ginger and Scallions

To make steamed Tilapia with ginger and scallions, you can follow these instructions:

Ingredients:

2 Tilapia fillets

1-inch piece of ginger, peeled and thinly sliced

2 scallions, sliced into long thin strips

2 tablespoons soy sauce

1 tablespoon sesame oil

1 tablespoon rice vinegar

Salt and pepper to taste

Instructions:

1. Rinse the Tilapia fillets under cold water and pat them dry with a paper towel. Season both sides of the fillets with salt and pepper.

2. Arrange a bed of ginger slices and scallion strips in a heatproof dish or on a steamer tray. Place the Tilapia fillets on top of the ginger and scallions.

3. In a small bowl, mix together the soy sauce, sesame oil, and rice vinegar. Pour this sauce mixture evenly over the Tilapia fillets, ensuring all parts are coated.

4. Fill a wok or a large pot with approximately 1-2 inches of water and place a steamer rack inside. Bring the water to a boil over high heat.

5. Once the water is boiling, carefully place the heatproof dish with the fish on the steamer rack. Cover the wok or pot with a lid and steam the Tilapia for about 8-10 minutes, or until the fish is opaque and

flakes easily with a fork. The cooking time may vary depending on the thickness of the fillets.

6. Once the Tilapia is steamed, remove the heatproof dish from the steamer and discard the ginger and scallions.

7. Serve the steamed Tilapia with ginger and scallions hot, garnished with additional sliced scallions. You can also drizzle some of the steaming sauce from the dish on top for added flavor.

This steamed Tilapia with ginger and scallions is a light and healthy dish that brings out the delicate flavors of the fish. Serve it with steamed rice and steamed vegetables for a complete meal. Enjoy!

Herb-Grilled Perch Tacos with Fresh Salsa

To make herb-grilled perch tacos with fresh salsa, follow these steps:

Ingredients for Herb-Grilled Perch:

1 pound perch fillets

2 tablespoons olive oil

2 tablespoons fresh herbs (such as parsley, cilantro, and dill), finely chopped

1 tablespoon lemon juice

Salt and pepper to taste

Ingredients for Fresh Salsa:

1 cup diced tomatoes

1/2 cup diced red onion

1/4 cup diced jalapeno (adjust to your preferred level of spiciness)

1/4 cup chopped fresh cilantro

1 tablespoon fresh lime juice

Salt and pepper to taste

Additional Taco Ingredients:

Tortillas (corn or flour)

Shredded lettuce

Sliced avocado

Sour cream (optional)

Lime wedges (for serving)

Instructions:

1. Preheat your grill to medium-high heat.

2. In a bowl, combine the olive oil, fresh herbs, lemon juice, salt, and pepper. Mix everything together to create a marinade for the perch.

3. Brush the marinade onto both sides of the perch fillets, ensuring they are well coated.

4. Place the marinated perch fillets on the preheated grill grates and cook for about 3-4 minutes per side, or until the fish is opaque and flakes easily with a fork. Cooking time may vary depending on the thickness of the fillets.

5. While the perch is grilling, prepare the fresh salsa. In a separate bowl, combine the diced tomatoes, red onion, jalapeno, chopped cilantro, lime juice, salt, and pepper. Mix everything together until well combined. Adjust the seasoning to your taste.

6. Once the perch is cooked, remove it from the grill and let it rest for a few minutes. Break the grilled fillets into smaller pieces.

7. Warm the tortillas in a dry skillet or on the grill for a minute or two on each side until they are pliable.

8. Assemble the tacos by placing some shredded lettuce on each tortilla. Top with the herb-grilled perch pieces, fresh salsa, sliced avocado, and any other desired toppings such as sour cream.

9. Squeeze fresh lime juice over the tacos for added tanginess.

Enjoy your herb-grilled perch tacos with fresh salsa! The combination of grilled fish, vibrant salsa, and toppings makes for a delicious and satisfying meal.

Poached Lake Bass with Lemon-Dill Sauce

To poach lake bass with lemon-dill sauce, follow these instructions:

Ingredients for Lake Bass:

2 lake bass fillets

2 cups fish or vegetable broth

1 lemon, sliced

Fresh dill sprigs
Salt and pepper to taste
<u>Ingredients for Lemon-Dill Sauce</u>:
1/2 cup mayonnaise
2 tablespoons fresh lemon juice
1 tablespoon finely chopped fresh dill
1 tablespoon Dijon mustard
Salt and pepper to taste
<u>Instructions</u>:
1. Pour the fish or vegetable broth into a large skillet or shallow pan. Place the lemon slices and a few sprigs of dill in the broth.

2. Season the lake bass fillets with salt and pepper on both sides.

3. Carefully place the seasoned bass fillets into the skillet, ensuring they are fully submerged in the broth.

4. Bring the broth to a gentle simmer over medium heat. Poach the bass fillets for about 10-12 minutes, or until the fish is opaque and flakes easily with a fork. Cooking time may vary based on the thickness of the fillets.

5. While the fish is poaching, prepare the lemon-dill sauce. In a small bowl, combine the mayonnaise, fresh lemon juice, chopped dill, Dijon mustard, salt, and pepper. Mix everything together until well combined. Taste and adjust the seasoning as needed.

6. Once the fish is cooked, carefully remove the fillets from the poaching liquid and transfer them to a serving plate.

7. Serve the poached lake bass hot, topped with a generous amount of the lemon-dill sauce.

You can pair the poached lake bass with steamed vegetables or a side of your choice for a complete meal. The delicate flavor of the fish, combined with the bright lemon-dill sauce, creates a tasty and elegant dish.

Chapter 8: Side Dishes and Accompaniments

Lemon-Herb Rice Pilaf

To make lemon-herb rice pilaf, follow these steps:

Ingredients:

1 cup long-grain rice

2 cups vegetable or chicken broth

1 tablespoon olive oil

1 small onion, finely chopped

2 cloves garlic, minced

Zest of 1 lemon

2 tablespoons lemon juice

1 tablespoon chopped fresh herbs (such as parsley, dill, or thyme)

Salt and pepper to taste

Instructions:

1. Rinse the rice under cold water until the water runs clear. Drain well.

2. In a saucepan, heat the olive oil over medium heat. Add the chopped onion and minced garlic. Sauté until the onion becomes translucent and the garlic is fragrant, usually about 2-3 minutes.

3. Add the rinsed rice to the saucepan and stir to coat the grains in the oil. Toast the rice for about 1-2 minutes to enhance its nutty flavor.

4. Pour in the vegetable or chicken broth, along with the lemon zest and lemon juice. Stir everything together.

5. Bring the mixture to a boil, then reduce the heat to low. Cover the saucepan with a tight-fitting lid and simmer for about 15-20

minutes, or until the rice is tender and the liquid is absorbed. Avoid removing the lid while the rice is cooking to ensure even cooking and fluffy results.

6. Once the rice is cooked, remove the saucepan from the heat and let it sit, covered, for another 5 minutes to allow the steam to finish cooking the rice.

7. Fluff the rice with a fork, then add the chopped fresh herbs. Mix everything together gently.

8. Season the lemon-herb rice pilaf with salt and pepper to taste. Adjust the seasoning as needed.

The lemon-herb rice pilaf is now ready to serve! This flavorful side dish pairs well with a variety of main dishes, from grilled chicken to roasted vegetables or seafood. Enjoy!

Grilled Asparagus with Parmesan

To make grilled asparagus with Parmesan, follow these steps:

Ingredients:

1 bunch of asparagus spears

2 tablespoons olive oil

Salt and pepper to taste

1/4 cup grated Parmesan cheese

1 tablespoon chopped fresh parsley (optional, for garnish)

Instructions:

1. Preheat your grill to medium-high heat.

2. Wash and trim the woody ends of the asparagus spears. If the spears are thick, you can peel the lower part with a vegetable peeler to ensure even cooking.

3. Place the asparagus spears in a large bowl and drizzle them with olive oil. Toss the asparagus to coat them evenly with the oil. Season with salt and pepper according to your taste.

4. Place the asparagus spears directly on the grill grates, perpendicular to the grates, if possible, to prevent them from falling

through. Grill the asparagus for about 5-7 minutes, turning occasionally, or until they are tender and have charred grill marks.

5. Sprinkle the grated Parmesan cheese evenly over the grilled asparagus spears. Close the grill lid and cook for an additional 1-2 minutes, or until the cheese has melted.

6. Remove the grilled asparagus from the grill and transfer them to a serving dish.

7. Garnish the grilled asparagus with chopped fresh parsley if desired.

Serve the grilled asparagus with Parmesan as a side dish alongside your favorite main course. It's a simple and delicious way to enjoy the natural flavors of asparagus with an added cheesy twist. Enjoy!

Creamy Coleslaw with Dill and Apple

To make creamy coleslaw with dill and apple, follow these steps:

Ingredients:

4 cups shredded cabbage (green or a combination of green and purple)

1 medium carrot, grated

1 green apple, julienned or grated

1/2 cup mayonnaise

1/4 cup sour cream

2 tablespoons apple cider vinegar

1 tablespoon Dijon mustard

1 tablespoon chopped fresh dill

1 teaspoon sugar or honey (optional)

Salt and pepper to taste

Instructions:

1. In a large bowl, combine the shredded cabbage, grated carrot, and julienned or grated green apple. Toss everything together until well mixed.

2. In a separate smaller bowl, whisk together the mayonnaise, sour cream, apple cider vinegar, Dijon mustard, chopped fresh dill, sugar or honey (optional), salt, and pepper. Adjust the seasoning to your taste.

3. Pour the dressing over the cabbage, carrot, and apple mixture. Use a spatula or large spoon to mix everything together until the vegetables are coated in the dressing.

4. Cover the bowl with plastic wrap or a lid and refrigerate for at least 1 hour to allow the flavors to meld together and the coleslaw to chill.

5. Before serving, give the coleslaw a final toss to ensure the dressing is evenly distributed.

Serve the creamy coleslaw with dill and apple as a refreshing side dish or as a topping for sandwiches and burgers. The combination of crisp cabbage, sweet apple, and tangy creamy dressing with a hint of dill creates a delicious balance of flavors. Enjoy!

Chapter 9: Sauces and Condiments

Tartar Sauce with Pickles and Capers

To make tartar sauce with pickles and capers, follow these steps:

Ingredients:

1 cup mayonnaise

2 tablespoons chopped pickles or pickle relish

1 tablespoon capers, drained and chopped

1 tablespoon finely chopped fresh parsley

1 tablespoon fresh lemon juice

1 teaspoon Dijon mustard

Salt and pepper to taste

Instructions:

1. In a small bowl, combine the mayonnaise, chopped pickles or pickle relish, chopped capers, finely chopped fresh parsley, lemon juice, and Dijon mustard. Mix everything together until well combined.

2. Taste the tartar sauce and season with salt and pepper according to your preference. Adjust the seasonings as needed.

3. Transfer the tartar sauce to a jar or container with a lid. Refrigerate for at least 30 minutes to allow the flavors to meld together.

4. Before serving, give the tartar sauce a good stir to ensure all the ingredients are evenly distributed.

Serve the tartar sauce with pickles and capers alongside seafood dishes such as fried fish, shrimp, or crab cakes. It adds a tangy and flavorful element to complement the richness of the seafood. Enjoy!

Homemade Cocktail Sauce

To make homemade cocktail sauce, follow these steps:

Ingredients:

1 cup ketchup

1 tablespoon horseradish (adjust to your preferred level of spiciness)

1 tablespoon fresh lemon juice

1 teaspoon Worcestershire sauce

Hot sauce (e.g., Tabasco or Tabanero), to taste (optional)

Salt and pepper to taste

Instructions:

1. In a bowl, combine the ketchup, horseradish, fresh lemon juice, and Worcestershire sauce. Stir everything together until well mixed.

2. Taste the sauce, and if desired, add hot sauce to add some heat. Adjust the level of spiciness based on your preference. Keep in mind that horseradish itself provides a bit of spiciness to the sauce.

3. Season the cocktail sauce with salt and pepper to taste. Adjust the seasoning as needed.

4. Transfer the cocktail sauce to a jar or container with a lid. Refrigerate for at least 30 minutes to allow the flavors to meld together.

Before serving, give the cocktail sauce a final stir. This homemade cocktail sauce pairs perfectly with shrimp, crab, or other seafood appetizers. Enjoy!

Beurre Blanc with White Wine and Shallots

To make Beurre Blanc with white wine and shallots, follow these steps:

Ingredients:

1/2 cup dry white wine

1/4 cup white wine vinegar

2 shallots, finely chopped

1/2 cup unsalted butter, cold and cut into small cubes

Salt and pepper to taste

Fresh lemon juice (optional)

<u>Instructions</u>:

1. In a small saucepan, combine the white wine, white wine vinegar, and chopped shallots. Bring the mixture to a simmer over medium heat. Allow it to reduce until only about 2 tablespoons of liquid remain, usually 8-10 minutes.

2. Once the liquid has reduced, reduce the heat to low and start whisking in the cold butter, a few cubes at a time. Whisk continuously, ensuring each addition of butter has melted and emulsified with the liquid before adding more. This will create a smooth and velvety texture.

3. Continue whisking in the butter until the sauce has thickened and achieved a slightly creamy consistency. Be patient and gradual with the process to prevent the sauce from separating.

4. Remove the saucepan from the heat and season the Beurre Blanc with Salt and pepper to taste. You can also add a squeeze of fresh lemon juice to brighten up the flavors. Adjust the seasoning and acidity to your taste.

5. Strain the sauce through a fine-mesh sieve to remove any remaining shallot pieces.

The Beurre Blanc sauce is now ready to serve. It pairs wonderfully with fish, shellfish, or roasted vegetables. Drizzle the sauce over your desired dish just before serving for an elegant and flavorful addition. Enjoy!

Chapter10: Desserts

Lemon Blueberry Cookies

Here's a recipe for lemon blueberry cookies:

Ingredients:

1/2 cup unsalted butter, softened

3/4 cup granulated sugar

1 tablespoon fresh lemon zest

1 tablespoon fresh lemon juice

1 teaspoon vanilla extract

1 large egg

1 3/4 cups all-purpose flour

1/2 teaspoon baking powder

1/4 teaspoon salt

1 cup fresh or frozen blueberries

Instructions:

1. Preheat your oven to 350°F (175°C) and line a baking sheet with parchment paper.

2. In a large mixing bowl, cream together the softened butter and granulated sugar until light and fluffy. You can use an electric mixer or do it by hand with a sturdy wooden spoon.

3. Add the lemon zest, lemon juice, vanilla extract, and egg to the butter-sugar mixture. Mix until well combined.

4. In a separate bowl, whisk together the all-purpose flour, baking powder, and salt. Gradually add the dry ingredients to the wet ingredients, mixing until just combined. Be careful not to overmix, as it can lead to tough cookies.

5. Gently fold in the blueberries, being careful not to crush them.

6. Drop spoonfuls of the cookie dough onto the prepared baking sheet, spacing them about 2 inches apart.

7. Bake the cookies in the preheated oven for approximately12-15 minutes, or until the edges are golden brown. The centers may still appear slightly soft, but they will firm up as the cookies cool.

8. Allow the cookies to cool on the baking sheet for a few minutes before transferring them to a wire rack to cool completely.

These lemon blueberry cookies are a delightful treat with a burst of fresh citrus flavor and juicy blueberries. Enjoy them with a cup of tea or as a sweet snack any time of the day!

<u>Grilled Pineapple with Honey and Cinnamon</u>

To make grilled pineapple with honey and cinnamon, follow these steps:

<u>Ingredients</u>:

1 fresh pineapple

2 tablespoons honey

1 teaspoon ground cinnamon

Optional: Vanilla ice cream or whipped cream for serving

<u>Instructions</u>:

1. Preheat your grill to medium heat.

2. Slice off the top, bottom, and outer peel of the pineapple. Cut the pineapple crosswise into half-inch-thick slices or into spears, depending on your preference.

3. In a small bowl, whisk together the honey and ground cinnamon until well combined.

4. Brush both sides of the pineapple slices or spears with the honey-cinnamon mixture, ensuring they are evenly coated.

5. Place the pineapple directly on the grill grates. Grill for about 2-3 minutes per side, or until the pineapple has nice grill marks and is heated through. Avoid cooking for too long, as the pineapple can become overly soft.

6. Once grilled, remove the pineapple from the grill and transfer it to a serving platter.

7. Serve the grilled pineapple as is or with a scoop of vanilla ice cream or a dollop of whipped cream if desired.

Grilled pineapple with honey and cinnamon offers a delightful combination of sweet, smoky, and warm flavors. Enjoy this delicious treat as a side dish or dessert at your next barbecue or cookout!

<u>Berry and Cream Crepes with Fresh Mint</u>

To make berry and cream crepes with fresh mint, follow these steps:

<u>Ingredients</u>:

For the crepes:

1 cup all-purpose flour

2 tablespoons granulated sugar

1/4 teaspoon salt

2 large eggs

11/4 cups milk

2 tablespoons melted butter

Additional butter for cooking

<u>For the filling</u>:

1 cup mixed berries (such as strawberries, blueberries, raspberries)

1 cup whipped cream or whipped topping

Fresh mint leaves for garnish

<u>Instructions</u>:

1. In a large mixing bowl, whisk together the flour, sugar, and salt. In a separate bowl, whisk together the eggs, milk, and melted butter.

2. Gradually pour the wet ingredients into the dry ingredients, whisking constantly, until a smooth batter is formed. Let the batter rest for approximately10 minutes to allow the flour to hydrate.

3. Heat a non-stick skillet or crepe pan over medium heat. Melt a small amount of butter in the pan and swirl it around to coat the surface.

4. Pour a small ladleful of batter into the pan, tilting the pan to spread the batter into a thin, even layer. Cook the crepe for about1-2 minutes, or until the edges start to turn golden brown.

5. Carefully flip the crepe using a spatula and cook for an additional 1-2 minutes on the other side. Repeat this process with the remaining batter, adding more butter to the pan as needed.

6. Once all the crepes are cooked, assemble the berry and cream crepes by spreading a thin layer of whipped cream or whipped topping on each crepe. Add a handful of mixed berries on top of the cream.

7. Roll or fold the crepes into a desired shape and arrange them on a serving plate.

8. Garnish the crepes with fresh mint leaves to add a refreshing touch.

Berry and cream crepes with fresh mint are a delectable and visually appealing treat. They are perfect for a brunch or dessert, and you can customize them with your favorite fruit and cream fillings. Enjoy!

Conclusion: But Not The End!

With the Weekend Fisherman's Cookbook, you have a treasure trove of recipes and techniques to turn your fishing endeavors into culinary successes. Remember, the key to a delicious meal is using fresh fish and exploring the diverse range of flavors and cooking methods available. Happy fishing and bon appétit!

BONUS BOOK

Empowered Survival: A Comprehensive Guide for Women

Introduction

The book, "Empowered Survival: A Comprehensive Guide for Women," aims to provide a thorough and empowering resource for women to enhance their survival skills in various situations. The purpose of the book is to equip women with the knowledge, tools, and mindset needed to navigate and overcome potential threats and challenges they might face in different aspects of life. The scope of the book encompasses a wide range of topics, including physical and mental preparedness, self-defense, home and personal security, urban and wilderness survival tactics, emergency first aid, emotional intelligence in survival, financial preparedness, technology and digital security, safe traveling, and post-survival recovery.

By offering practical advice, step-by-step guides, and real-world strategies, the book intends to empower women to take control of their safety and well-being. It recognizes the diverse situations women may encounter and provides tailored insights to address those specific needs. The overarching goal is to foster a sense of self-reliance, confidence, and resilience, ultimately contributing to a safer and more secure future for women in various environments and circumstances.

Empowerment and self-reliance for women are crucial components of personal development and societal progress. Here are some key reasons highlighting their importance:

1. <u>Personal Safety and Well-being</u>:

Empowered women are more likely to be aware of potential risks and take proactive measures to ensure their safety. This includes physical, emotional, and financial well-being.

2. Enhanced Confidence and Resilience:

Empowerment fosters a sense of self-confidence and resilience. Women who feel empowered are better equipped to face challenges, overcome obstacles, and bounce back from setbacks.

3. Equality and Social Justice:

Empowering women contributes to the overall goal of gender equality. When women are self-reliant and empowered, they are better positioned to advocate for their rights and contribute to dismantling systemic inequalities.

4. Improved Decision-Making:

Empowered women tend to be more assertive and decisive in making choices that affect their lives. This extends to various aspects such as career decisions, relationships, and personal goals.

5. Economic Independence:

Self-reliance is often linked to economic independence. When women have the skills and confidence to support themselves financially, they are less vulnerable to economic exploitation and more capable of making choices aligned with their values and goals.

6. Positive Role Modeling:

Empowered women serve as positive role models for others, inspiring and encouraging future generations. This contributes to a cultural shift toward recognizing and valuing the strengths and contributions of women in society.

7. Community Impact:

Empowered and self-reliant women positively impact their communities. They are more likely to engage in community development, share knowledge, and contribute to social progress.

8. Health and Well-being:

Empowered women often prioritize their health and well-being. This includes seeking medical care, adopting healthy lifestyles, and making informed choices about their physical and mental health.

9. Educational Attainment:

-Empowerment is closely linked to educational opportunities. When women are encouraged to pursue education and skill development, they are better equipped to navigate various aspects of life.

10. Agency and Autonomy:

-Empowerment gives women a sense of agency and autonomy over their lives. This involves having control over their choices, resources, and the ability to shape their own destinies.

In summary, empowerment and self-reliance for women are foundational elements for personal growth, societal progress, and the achievement of gender equality. By fostering these qualities, individuals and communities contribute to a more just, equitable, and resilient world.

Brief statistics on women's safety concerns

While the specific statistics may vary depending on the region and context, here are some general statistics highlighting women's safety concerns:

1. Violence Against Women:

According to the World Health Organization (WHO), about 1 in 3 women worldwide has experienced either physical or sexual intimate partner violence or non-partner sexual violence in their lifetime.

2. Sexual Assault:

In many countries, a significant percentage of women report experiencing sexual assault during their lifetime. This includes incidents of rape, attempted rape, and other forms of sexual violence.

3. Human Trafficking:

Women and girls make up a significant portion of human trafficking victims, subjected to forced labor, sexual exploitation, and other forms of abuse.

4. Domestic Violence:

Domestic violence remains a pervasive issue, with a substantial number of women facing physical, emotional, or economic abuse within intimate relationships.

5. <u>Cyber Harassment</u>:

The rise of digital technology has led to an increase in cyber harassment and online abuse, affecting many women globally.

6. <u>Workplace Harassment</u>:

Women continue to face challenges related to workplace harassment, including sexual harassment and discrimination.

7. <u>Unequal Access to Education</u>:

In some regions, cultural norms and societal expectations limit women's access to education, impacting their ability to empower themselves and participate fully in society.

8. <u>Limited Economic Opportunities</u>:

Women often face barriers in accessing economic opportunities, including gender pay gaps, limited job opportunities, and obstacles to entrepreneurship.

9. <u>Maternal Health</u>:

Maternal health concerns, including lack of access to proper healthcare during pregnancy and childbirth, contribute to safety issues for women in certain regions.

10. <u>Child Marriage and Female Genital Mutilation (FGM)</u>:

Harmful practices such as child marriage and FGM continue to affect the safety and well-being of women, particularly in some communities and cultures.

It's important to note that addressing women's safety concerns requires a multi-faceted approach involving legal, social, and cultural changes. Awareness, education, and empowerment initiatives play crucial roles in combating these issues and creating safer environments for women.

Chapter 1: Understanding the threat landscape

DIFFERENT FORMS OF threats and risks: Bugging out

"Bugging out" refers to the act of leaving one's home or current location quickly and urgently, often in response to a threatening or dangerous situations. While the need to "bug out" can apply to anyone, regardless of gender, women may find themselves in situations where this becomes a necessary course of action due to various threats. Here are some reasons why a woman might need to "bug out":

1. Natural Disasters:

Women, like anyone else, may need to evacuate in the face of natural disasters such as hurricanes, floods, wildfires, earthquakes, or tornadoes. Quick evacuation can be essential for personal safety.

2. Civil Unrest or Political Instability:

Political upheaval, civil unrest, or situations of political instability can pose risks to personal safety. In such cases, individuals may need to leave their homes temporarily until the situation stabilizes.

3. Domestic Violence:

Women experiencing domestic violence may need to "bug out" to escape an abusive situation quickly and find a safe haven. This could involve leaving a shared residence to seek refuge in a shelter or with a trusted friend.

4. Threats to Personal Safety:

Personal threats from individuals, such as stalking, harassment, or violence, may necessitate a woman quickly leaving her current location to protect herself and seek a safer environment.

5. Public Health Emergencies:

Situations like pandemics or the outbreak of contagious diseases may require individuals, including women, to relocate temporarily to minimize exposure and ensure personal safety.

6. Evacuation Orders:

Authorities may issue evacuation orders due to various emergencies, including environmental hazards, industrial accidents, or other threats. Women would need to follow these orders to ensure their safety.

7. Terrorist Threats:

In situations involving potential terrorist threats or attacks, individuals may need to evacuate certain areas quickly to avoid harm.

8. Financial Instability:

Economic crises or sudden financial instability may force individuals, including women, to leave their homes in search of better economic opportunities or more stable living conditions.

9. Family Protection:

Women may need to bug out to protect their children or other family members in emergency situations. Ensuring the safety of dependents is a primary concern in such cases.

10. Animal Attacks or Environmental Threats:

In certain outdoor or rural environments, women might need to evacuate quickly to escape threats such as aggressive wildlife, environmental hazards, or other dangers.

It's important to note that the decision to "bug out" is a complex one and depends on the specific circumstances. Preparedness, including having a plan, emergency supplies, and knowledge of evacuation routes, is crucial for both men and women to respond effectively to various threats and emergencies.

The psychological impact of fear on survival

The psychological impact of fear can significantly influence a woman's ability to survive during a crisis. Understanding these effects is crucial for developing strategies to cope with and overcome fear in emergency situations. Here are some key aspects of the psychological impact of fear on survival for women:

1. <u>Impaired Decision-Making:</u>

Fear triggers the body's "fight or flight" response, flooding the system with stress hormones. This physiological reaction can impair cognitive functions, making it challenging for women to think clearly and make rational decisions during a crisis.

2. <u>Heightened Anxiety and Stress</u>:

Prolonged exposure to fear and uncertainty can lead to heightened anxiety and stress. Chronic stress can negatively impact mental and physical well-being, affecting a woman's ability to cope with and adapt to the challenges of a survival situation.

3. <u>Impact on Physical Health</u>:

The psychological stress induced by fear can manifest in physical symptoms, such as increased heart rate, muscle tension, headaches, and gastrointestinal issues. These physical responses can further contribute to the overall sense of vulnerability and hinder effective survival actions.

4. <u>Disruption of Focus and Attention</u>:

Fear can cause a narrowing of attention, focusing on the perceived threat while disregarding other important information. This tunnel vision can limit a woman's ability to assess her surroundings, gather information, and make well-informed decisions during a crisis.

5. <u>Paralysis and Inaction</u>:

Intense fear may lead to a state of paralysis, where a woman becomes emotionally overwhelmed and unable to take necessary actions for survival. This response can hinder the ability to escape danger or address immediate threats.

6. <u>Impact on Interpersonal Relationships</u>:

Fear can strain interpersonal relationships, affecting communication and collaboration. In a crisis, effective teamwork and cooperation are vital, and fear-induced stress may hinder the ability to work together with others for mutual survival.

7. <u>Long-Term Psychological Trauma</u>:

Experiencing fear during a crisis can lead to long-term psychological trauma. Women may develop post-traumatic stress disorder (PTSD) or other mental health issues, impacting their overall well-being and resilience in future situations.

8. <u>Coping Mechanisms and Emotional Regulation</u>:

Developing effective coping mechanisms and emotional regulation skills is essential. Women who can manage fear and stress through healthy coping strategies, such as deep breathing, mindfulness, or positive self-talk, are better equipped to navigate challenging situations.

9. <u>Importance of Training and Preparedness</u>:

Training and preparedness can help mitigate the psychological impact of fear. Women who have undergone relevant training are more likely to respond calmly and effectively during a crisis, as they have acquired the skills and knowledge needed for survival.

10. <u>Cultivating Resilience</u>:

Building resilience is crucial for overcoming fear and adversity. Women can develop resilience through mental preparedness, self-awareness, and a positive mindset, enabling them to adapt and recover from stressful situations more effectively.

In summary, understanding the psychological impact of fear on women during a crisis emphasizes the importance of both psychological preparedness and the cultivation of resilience to enhance survival outcomes.

Chapter 2: Developing a Survival Mindset

IMPORTANCE OF A POSITIVE mindset in survival situations

A positive mindset is crucial for women in survival situations, as it plays a significant role in shaping their thoughts, emotions, and actions. Here are key reasons highlighting the importance of a positive mindset in survival situations for women:

1. Enhanced Decision-Making:

A positive mindset enables clearer and more rational decision-making. It helps women focus on solutions rather than dwelling on the severity of the situation, leading to better-informed and more effective choices.

2. Increased Resilience:

Positivity fosters resilience, allowing women to bounce back from challenges, setbacks, and adversity. Resilience is essential for enduring difficult circumstances and adapting to changes in the survival environment.

3. Stress Reduction:

Maintaining a positive outlook helps reduce stress and anxiety. In survival situations, stress management is crucial for optimal cognitive functioning, physical health, and emotional well-being.

4. Optimism and Hope:

Optimism and hope are powerful motivators. A positive mindset instills a belief that challenges can be overcome and that there is a path to a better outcome. This optimism can drive perseverance and determination.

5. Improved Problem-Solving Skills:

A positive mindset enhances creativity and problem-solving skills. Women with a positive outlook are more likely to approach challenges with a solution-oriented mindset, thinking outside the box to find innovative ways to address problems.

6. Social Connection and Teamwork:

Positivity fosters stronger social connections. In survival situations, teamwork and collaboration are often critical. A positive mindset promotes cooperation, communication, and mutual support among individuals facing a common challenge.

7. Physical Health Benefits:

Positive emotions have been linked to better physical health. Maintaining a positive mindset can contribute to overall well-being, which is essential for enduring the physical demands of survival situations.

8. Adaptability and Flexibility:

A positive mindset facilitates adaptability and flexibility. Women who approach challenges with optimism are more likely to adapt to changing circumstances, embrace new strategies, and find opportunities for growth in adversity.

9. Mind-Body Connection:

The mind-body connection is powerful. Positive thoughts can have a beneficial impact on physical well-being, potentially improving endurance, pain tolerance, and overall physical resilience.

10. Empowerment and Self-Efficacy:

A positive mindset enhances feelings of empowerment and self-efficacy. Women who believe in their ability to navigate challenges are more likely to take proactive steps toward survival and engage in behaviors that contribute to their well-being.

11. Visualization exercises and mindfulness techniques

When it comes to visualization exercises and mindfulness techniques for women in survival circumstances, there are several helpful practices you can consider. These techniques can support your mental well-being and help you stay grounded during challenging situations.

<u>Here are a few suggestions:</u>

<u>1. Grounding Exercises</u>:

Start by finding a quiet and safe space. Take deep breaths and focus on your breath, feeling each inhale and exhale. Gradually direct your attention to your body. Notice the sensations in your feet, legs, hands, and other parts of your body. This practice can help you feel more connected to your physical surroundings and provide a sense of stability.

2. <u>Guided Imagery</u>:

Close your eyes and imagine yourself in a calm and serene environment. Picture a place where you feel safe, secure, and at peace. It can be a beach, a forest, or any location that brings you comfort. Engage all your senses as you visualize the sounds, smells, and textures of that place. This exercise can transport your mind to a peaceful mental space.

3. <u>Positive Affirmations</u>:

Repeat positive affirmations to yourself, focusing on your strength, resilience, and ability to overcome challenges. These affirmations can help boost your confidence and remind you of your inner power. Choose statements that resonate with you, such as "I am strong," "I am capable," or "I can handle whatever comes my way."

4. <u>Mindful Breathing</u>:

Paying attention to your breath can bring you into the present moment and help you find calm and clarity. Place your hand on your belly and take slow, deep breaths, feeling your abdomen rise and fall. As you breathe, focus solely on the sensation of breathing in and out. If your mind wanders, gently bring your attention back to your breath.

5. <u>Journaling</u>:

Writing down your thoughts and emotions can be a powerful way to process your experiences. Find a journal or a piece of paper and express your thoughts, fears, and hopes. You can also write down any positive moments or acts of kindness you've witnessed or experienced. Journaling can offer a cathartic outlet and promote self-reflection.

In summary, a positive mindset is a valuable asset for women in survival situations. It not only improves mental and emotional well-being but also contributes to better decision-making, resilience, and the ability to adapt to challenging circumstances. Cultivating and maintaining a positive outlook can significantly enhance a woman's chances of survival and overall well-being in emergency situations.

Chapter 3: Physical Preparedness

BASIC SELF-DEFENSE techniques

Empowering women with basic self-defense techniques is crucial for enhancing personal safety. While self-defense training is comprehensive and best learned through practical instruction, here are some fundamental principles and techniques that women can consider:

1. Awareness and Avoidance:

Stay aware of your surroundings and trust your instincts. Avoid potentially risky situations when possible and be mindful of your environment.

2. Maintain Distance:

Keep a safe distance from strangers, especially in isolated or unfamiliar areas. Creating space provides more time to react if a threat arises.

3. Use Verbal Assertiveness:

Project confidence through assertive verbal communication. Clearly communicate boundaries and let others know when they are making you uncomfortable.

4. Learn Basic Strikes:

Practice basic strikes to vulnerable areas, such as the eyes, nose, throat, and groin. Techniques like palm strikes, knee strikes, and elbow strikes can be effective in creating openings for escape.

5. Escape Holds and Grabs:

Learn techniques to escape common holds and grabs, such as wrist grabs or bear hugs. Utilize leverage, joint manipulation, and quick movements to break free.

6. Practice Ground Defense:

If taken to the ground, practice techniques to defend yourself. This may include escapes from holds or learning how to get back on your feet quickly.

7. Use Everyday Objects:

Learn to use everyday objects as improvised self-defense tools. Items like keys, pens, or umbrellas can be effective in creating a distraction or fending off an attacker.

8. Focus on Key Vulnerabilities:

Identify key vulnerabilities on the human body, such as pressure points and sensitive areas. Targeting these areas can be effective in incapacitating an assailant temporarily.

9. Take a Self-Defense Class:

Consider enrolling in a self-defense class specifically designed for women. In-person classes provide hands-on experience and guidance from trained instructors.

10. Practice Situational Awareness:

Be aware of your surroundings and potential escape routes. Understanding the environment can help you make quick and effective decisions in a threatening situation.

11. Use Your Voice:

Shout loudly to attract attention and create a scene if you feel threatened. This can deter an attacker and alert others to your situation.

12. Stay Fit:

Physical fitness enhances your ability to execute self-defense techniques effectively. Regular exercise improves strength, agility, and overall physical preparedness.

Remember that the goal of self-defense is to create an opportunity to escape safely. Continual practice and reinforcement of these techniques, ideally through professional instruction, can help build muscle memory and confidence in applying these skills when needed. Additionally, self-defense is not just physical; it includes mental and emotional aspects, such as situational awareness and the ability to remain calm under pressure.

Fitness and strength training for optimal readiness

Fitness and strength training are essential components of women's preparedness, contributing to overall health, resilience, and the ability to respond effectively in various situations. Here are key considerations and guidelines for women's fitness and strength training to achieve optimal readiness:

1. Cardiovascular Exercise:

-Engage in regular cardiovascular exercise to improve endurance and cardiovascular health. Activities like running, brisk walking, cycling, and swimming are effective for enhancing overall fitness.

2. Strength Training:

Incorporate strength training into your routine to build muscle strength. Focus on compound exercises that target multiple muscle groups, such as squats, deadlifts, bench presses, and pull-ups.

3. Functional Training:

Emphasize functional training that mimics real-life movements. This type of training enhances overall agility, balance, and coordination, which are valuable in emergency situations.

4. Core Strength:

Strengthen the core muscles to improve stability and support the spine. Core exercises like planks, Russian twists, and leg raises contribute to a strong and stable midsection.

5. Flexibility and Mobility:

Include flexibility and mobility exercises to maintain joint health and prevent injuries. Yoga and dynamic stretching can enhance overall flexibility.

6. Interval Training:

Incorporate interval training into your workouts to improve both cardiovascular fitness and endurance. High-intensity interval training (HIIT) is effective for burning calories and improving overall fitness.

7. <u>Balance and Coordination:</u>

Practice exercises that enhance balance and coordination. This can include activities like stability exercises, balance drills, and agility training.

8. <u>Bodyweight Exercises:</u>

Include bodyweight exercises in your routine, as they can be performed anywhere and are effective for building strength. Examples include push-ups, squats, lunges, and burpees.

9. <u>Cross-Training:</u>

Engage in cross-training to prevent boredom and avoid overuse injuries. Incorporate a variety of exercises and activities to challenge different muscle groups and energy systems.

10. <u>Consistency is Key:</u>

Establish a consistent workout routine. Regular physical activity contributes to long-term health benefits and ensures that you are physically prepared for unexpected challenges.

11. <u>Functional Strength for Everyday Tasks:</u>

-Tailor strength training to enhance functional strength for everyday tasks. Consider exercises that simulate lifting, carrying, and pushing to prepare for real-life scenarios.

12. <u>Listen to Your Body:</u>

-Pay attention to your body's signals. If you experience pain or discomfort, modify exercises as needed, and consult with a fitness professional or healthcare provider if necessary.

13. <u>Hydration and Nutrition:</u>

Stay well-hydrated and maintain a balanced diet to support your fitness goals. Proper nutrition is crucial for energy, recovery, and overall well-being.

14. <u>Rest and Recovery:</u>

Allow sufficient time for rest and recovery. Adequate sleep and rest days between intense workouts are essential for preventing overtraining and promoting overall health.

Remember that individual fitness levels vary, and it's important to tailor a fitness and strength training program to your specific needs and goals. Consult with a fitness professional or healthcare provider before starting a new exercise regimen, especially if you have pre-existing health conditions or concerns.

Chapter 4: Home Security and Personal Safety

SECURING YOUR LIVING space

Securing your living space is a critical aspect of women's home security and personal safety. Here are practical strategies and tips to enhance the security of your home:

1. Install Strong Doors and Locks:

Invest in solid doors made of materials like metal or solid wood. Install high-quality deadbolt locks on exterior doors to reinforce entry points.

2. Upgrade Windows:

Install window locks to prevent easy access. Consider using laminated or tempered glass to make it more difficult for intruders to break in.

3. Use Security Cameras:

Install security cameras at key entry points and around the perimeter of your home. Visible cameras act as a deterrent, while hidden cameras can capture footage discreetly.

4. Exterior Lighting:

Ensure adequate exterior lighting to eliminate dark areas around your home. Motion-activated lights are effective in deterring intruders and alerting you to potential threats.

5. Trim Landscaping:

Keep shrubs, trees, and bushes well-trimmed to eliminate hiding spots for potential intruders. This enhances visibility around your property.

6. <u>Secure Garage Doors</u>:

Ensure that garage doors are secure, as they can be vulnerable entry points. Use sturdy locks and consider a security system for your garage.

7. <u>Reinforce Sliding Doors</u>:

Install a security bar or rod in the track of sliding doors to prevent forced entry. Consider using reinforced glass or laminates for added protection.

8. <u>Home Security System</u>:

Invest in a reliable home security system that includes door/window sensors, motion detectors, and alarms. Many modern systems offer remote monitoring through mobile apps.

9. <u>Secure Valuables</u>:

Keep valuables in a secure, hidden location or invest in a safe. This prevents easy access to important documents, jewelry, and other valuable items.

10. <u>Establish a Neighborhood Watch</u>:

Participate in or establish a neighborhood watch program. Collaborate with neighbors to look out for each other and share information about suspicious activity.

11. <u>Change Locks Regularly</u>:

If you move into a new home or misplace your keys, change the locks immediately. This ensures that you are the only person with access to your home.

12. <u>Use Timers for Lights</u>:

Install timers on lights, radios, or TVs to create the illusion of an occupied home when you're away. This can deter potential burglars.

13. <u>Know Your Neighbors</u>:

Build good relationships with your neighbors. Having a network of trustworthy neighbors can enhance overall safety and security.

14. <u>Emergency Preparedness Kit</u>:

Prepare an emergency kit with essentials like flashlights, first aid supplies, and important documents (in a fireproof receptacle). Keep everything in an easily accessible location.

15. <u>Personal Safety Measures</u>:

Practice personal safety measures, such as being cautious when opening the door to strangers, not publicizing your absence on social media, and being vigilant about unexpected visitors.

Remember that home security is a multi-faceted approach. It's essential to combine technology, physical barriers, and personal awareness to create a comprehensive security plan for your living space. Regularly assess and update your security measures to adapt to changing circumstances and technologies.

<u>Choosing and using personal safety devices</u>

Choosing and using personal safety devices can be an effective part of a woman's overall safety strategy. Here are some considerations for selecting and utilizing personal safety devices:

1. <u>Personal Alarm</u>:

<u>Choosing</u>: Select a personal alarm that emits a loud, attention-grabbing sound. Look for a device that is easy to carry and activate quickly.

<u>Using</u>: Keep the personal alarm easily accessible, such as on a keychain or in a pocket. In an emergency, activate the alarm to attract attention and deter potential threats.

2. <u>Pepper Spray or Mace</u>:

<u>Choosing</u>: Choose a reliable pepper spray or mace product with a high concentration of the active ingredient. Ensure it has a secure safety mechanism to prevent accidental discharge.

<u>Using</u>: Familiarize yourself with the proper way to use the spray, including the range and direction. Keep it readily available, but use it responsibly and in accordance with local laws.

3. <u>Stun Guns or Tasers</u>:

<u>Choosing</u>: If legal and appropriate in your area, select a stun gun or Taser from a reputable manufacturer. Ensure it has safety features to prevent accidental discharge.

<u>Using</u>: Learn how to use the device properly, including understanding its range and limitations. Use it only in situations where it is legally and ethically justified.

4. <u>Safety Whistle</u>:

<u>Choosing</u>: Opt for a durable and loud safety whistle. Consider one with multiple tones or features for added versatility.

<u>Using</u>: Keep the whistle easily accessible. In emergencies, use the whistle to signal for help or to draw attention to your location.

5. <u>Personal Safety Apps</u>:

<u>Choosing</u>: Explore personal safety apps that offer features like location tracking, emergency contacts, and distress signals. Choose an app that aligns with your needs and preferences.

<u>Using</u>: Keep your phone charged and the app activated. Familiarize yourself with its features, especially those that can quickly alert contacts or emergency services.

6. <u>Self-Defense Keychain Tools</u>:

<u>Choosing</u>: Some keychain tools are designed for self-defense, such as kubotans or cat-shaped keychains. Choose a tool that suits your comfort level and local regulations.

<u>Using</u>: Practice using the tool in a controlled environment. Keep it within reach, and use it strategically if faced with a threatening situation.

7. <u>Smart Safety Jewelry</u>:

<u>Choosing</u>: Consider smart safety jewelry that includes features like GPS tracking, emergency alerts, or distress signals. Choose a style that aligns with your preferences.

-<u>Using</u>: Ensure the device is charged and activated. Familiarize yourself with the features and use them as needed in emergency situations.

8. <u>Wearable Safety Devices</u>:

<u>Choosing</u>: Wearable safety devices, such as smartwatches with safety features, are available. Choose a device that integrates well with your lifestyle and provides the functionalities you need.

<u>Using</u>: Wear the device regularly and activate its safety features when necessary. Ensure it is charged and synced with your smartphone or other devices.

Remember to check and comply with local laws and regulations regarding the possession and use of personal safety devices. Training and familiarization with these devices are essential for effective and responsible use in emergency situations.

<u>Creating a safety plan for various scenarios</u>

Creating a comprehensive safety plan for various scenarios is a proactive approach to personal security. The plan should address a range of situations, from everyday concerns to emergencies. Here's a general guide to help women develop a safety plan:

1. <u>Home Security</u>:

-Install strong doors, locks, and windows.

-Have a reliable home security system.

-Keep entry points well-lit.

-Don't publicize vacations on social media.

-Know your neighbors and establish a community watch if possible.

2. <u>Personal Safety While Out</u>:

-Be aware of your surroundings.

-Trust your instincts; if something feels off, take precautions.

-Avoid poorly lit areas, especially at night.

-Use well-traveled routes.

-Share your itinerary with a trusted friend or family member.

3. <u>Workplace Safety</u>:

-Be aware of emergency exits.

-Report any suspicious activity to security.

-Keep personal information private.

-Have a designated contact for emergencies.

-If working late, inform someone of your schedule.

4. <u>Transportation Safety</u>:

-Keep your vehicle well-maintained.

-Lock doors while driving.

-Have a reliable roadside assistance plan.

-Use well-lit and populated parking areas.

-Share your transportation plans with someone.

5. <u>Online and Digital Safety</u>:

-Use strong, unique passwords.

-Be cautious about sharing personal information online.

-Regularly update software and antivirus programs.

-Enable two-factor authentication where possible.

-Monitor bank and online accounts for unusual activity.

6. <u>Emergency Evacuation</u>:

-Know escape routes in your home and workplace.

-Have a designated meeting place for family or colleagues.

-Keep important documents in a secure, easily accessible place.

-Have an emergency kit with essentials.

-Stay informed about local emergency procedures.

7. <u>Medical Emergencies</u>:

-Keep a list of emergency contacts.

-Carry a small medical information card.

-Know the location of the nearest medical facilities.

-Inform others about any allergies or medical conditions.

-Learn basic first aid and CPR.

8. <u>Natural Disasters</u>:

-Familiarize yourself with local evacuation routes.

-Have an emergency kit with essentials.

-Create a family communication plan.

-Stay informed about weather alerts and warnings.

-Establish emergency contacts outside your area.

9. <u>Domestic Violence or Harassment</u>:

-Have a safe place to go if needed.

-Inform a trusted friend or family member about your situation.

-Develop a code word or signal to communicate distress discreetly.

-Keep important documents in a safe location.

-Seek assistance from local support organizations.

10. <u>Travel Safety</u>:

-Research and be aware of local customs and laws.

-Share your travel itinerary with someone.

-Keep valuables secure and be cautious of pickpockets.

-Have emergency contact information for local authorities.

-Be cautious about sharing travel plans on social media.

<u>Additional Tips</u>:

Practice situational awareness regularly.

Stay updated on self-defense techniques.

Attend personal safety workshops or classes.

Review and update your safety plan periodically.

Trust your instincts and intuition.

Customize this safety plan based on your specific needs, lifestyle, and location. Regularly review and practice your plan to ensure readiness in various scenarios. Remember, the key is to be proactive and prepared, promoting a sense of empowerment and confidence in navigating different situations.

Chapter 5: Urban Survival Tactics

NAVIGATING AND SURVIVING in urban environments

Navigating and surviving in urban environments requires a combination of awareness, preparedness, and practical strategies. Here are some tips for women to navigate and enhance their safety in urban settings:

1. Be Aware of Your Surroundings:

Stay alert and aware of your surroundings at all times.

Limit distractions such as excessive phone use, especially in unfamiliar or dimly lit areas.

2. Plan Your Route:

Choose well-lit and populated routes, especially at night.

Familiarize yourself with the layout of the city and know alternative routes.

3. Use Public Transportation Safely:

Be cautious when waiting for public transportation, especially late at night.

Wait in well-lit and busy areas.

Know the schedule and routes in advance.

4. Travel in Groups:

Whenever possible, travel with friends or in groups.

There is safety in numbers, and potential attackers are less likely to target a group.

5. Share Your Plans:

Inform someone you trust about your plans and whereabouts.

Use apps that allow you to share your location with trusted contacts.

6. <u>Carry Essentials</u>:

Keep only essential items in your purse or bag.

Carry a fully charged phone, a small flashlight, and personal safety devices if legally allowed.

7. <u>Use Well-Lit Areas</u>:

Stick to well-lit streets, especially after dark.

Avoid shortcuts through alleys or poorly lit areas.

8. <u>Trust Your Instincts</u>:

If something feels off, trust your instincts and take precautions.

Change your route or seek assistance if you feel uncomfortable.

9. <u>Learn Self-Defense</u>:

Take self-defense classes to learn basic techniques for personal safety.

Practice situational awareness and avoidance strategies.

10. <u>Secure Your Home</u>:

Ensure that your home is secure with strong locks and doors.

Use window coverings to prevent outsiders from seeing inside.

11. <u>Know Emergency Contacts</u>:

Save emergency contacts in your phone, including local authorities and trusted friends or family members.

12. <u>Avoid Displaying Valuables:</u>

Keep valuable items like jewelry and electronics out of sight.

Use discreet bags or backpacks when carrying valuable items.

13. <u>Be Cautious with Strangers</u>:

Avoid engaging with strangers in isolated areas.

Trust your instincts and be cautious about sharing personal information.

14. <u>Stay Informed</u>:

Stay updated on local news and events that may impact your safety.

Be aware of any safety alerts or advisories in your area.

15. <u>Utilize Safe Transportation Options</u>:

Choose reputable and licensed transportation services.

Use well-known rideshare services and confirm the driver's identity before entering the vehicle.

16. <u>Blend In</u>:

Dress in a way that helps you blend in with the local population.

Avoid drawing unnecessary attention to yourself.

17. <u>Know Safe Places</u>:

Identify safe places, such as police stations, hospitals, or businesses that are open late, along your route.

18. <u>Attend Personal Safety Workshops</u>:

Attend workshops or classes focused on personal safety and urban survival.

19. <u>Carry Identification</u>:

Always carry identification with you, and consider having an emergency contact card in your wallet.

20. <u>Trust Your Network</u>-Develop a network of trusted friends, neighbors, or coworkers who can provide support and assistance when needed.

Remember, personal safety is a dynamic aspect of urban living, and adapting to different situations is essential. Regularly reassess and update your safety practices to align with your lifestyle and the changing urban environment.

Blending in and avoiding attention

<u>Emergency urban shelters and resources</u>

In urban environments, there are often emergency shelters and resources available to provide support in times of crisis. Women should be aware of these options to ensure their safety and well-being. Here are some key resources:

1.<u>Local Emergency Shelters:</u>

Familiarize yourself with local emergency shelters in your city or town. These shelters may be activated during natural disasters, extreme weather events, or other emergencies. Contact local authorities or check community resources for information on the nearest shelters.

2. <u>Domestic Violence Shelters</u>:

Domestic violence shelters provide a safe haven for women escaping abusive situations. They offer confidential and supportive services, including counseling, legal assistance, and resources to help survivors rebuild their lives. In the U.S., the National Domestic Violence Hotline (1-800-799-SAFE) can provide information on shelters and support services.

3. <u>Women's Crisis Centers</u>:

Women's crisis centers are community-based organizations that offer support to women facing various crises, including domestic violence, sexual assault, and homelessness. These centers may provide temporary shelter, counseling, legal advocacy, and other resources.

4. <u>Homeless Shelters</u>:

Homeless shelters provide temporary accommodation for individuals experiencing homelessness. Some shelters may have specific accommodations or programs for women, offering a safe place to sleep, meals, and access to hygiene facilities.

5. <u>Community Outreach Programs</u>:

Many urban areas have community outreach programs that provide resources and support to individuals in need. These programs may offer assistance with food, clothing, and housing. Local community centers, churches, or nonprofit organizations often coordinate these efforts.

6. <u>Emergency Hotlines</u>:

Be aware of emergency hotlines that provide immediate assistance and information. In addition to the National Domestic Violence Hotline, other hotlines may offer support for various crises, including mental health emergencies, sexual assault, and homelessness.

7. <u>Legal Aid and Advocacy Services</u>:

Legal aid services and advocacy organizations can assist women in navigating legal issues related to domestic violence, harassment, or other crises. They may provide legal representation, advice, and resources to help women understand and assert their rights.

8. <u>Local Government and Social Services</u>:

Contact your local government's social services department for information on available resources. This may include housing assistance, food programs, and emergency financial aid.

9. <u>Healthcare Facilities</u>:

Hospitals and community health clinics can be resources for women in need of medical assistance or support. Some healthcare facilities also have social workers who can connect individuals with relevant services.

10. <u>Community Support Groups</u>:

Joining community support groups can provide emotional support and information on available resources. These groups may be facilitated by local organizations or conducted online.

11. <u>Transportation Services</u>:

Some urban areas offer transportation services to help individuals access shelters and support services. Know the availability and contact information for these services in your area.

12. <u>Online Resources and Apps</u>:

Explore online resources and mobile apps that provide information about local shelters, crisis centers, and support services. Some apps offer features like safety planning and emergency alerts.

13. <u>Employer Assistance Programs</u>:

Check if your employer has assistance programs that can provide support during challenging times. These programs may include counseling services, financial assistance, or referrals to community resources.

14. <u>Educational Institutions</u>:

If you are a student, check with your educational institution for support services. Many universities and colleges have resources for students facing crises, including counseling services and emergency assistance programs.

Being aware of these resources and having a plan in place can empower women to seek help and support when needed. It's important to share this information with others, including friends, family, and colleagues, to create a supportive network in the community.

Want to read more? Buy EMPOWERED SURVIVAL from your favorite outlet.

BONUS #2

No Second Chances
Historical Romance

CHAPTER ONE

Her head hurt. That was the first conscious thought that she formed. A throbbing, living pain, with its own agenda apparently, it seemed to begin above her left eyebrow and radiate out into whatever direction it gleefully chose to take. Assigning it a will of its own was the only way she could step aside from it and, by doing so, lessen its hold on her. She let one eye open slightly and when the pain did not increase, she indulged herself in opening the other.

"She's awake!" came a strained whisper from somewhere nearby. "Tell 'is Lordship! 'urry off wid' ye now!" the voice finished.

Since she couldn't tell a great deal about her surroundings with her eyes only slightly open, she allowed them to flutter open a little more. The first impression she had was how rich the room looked. With velvet bed hangings and curtains, silk-draped walls, crystal vases filled with roses, a velvet upholstered settee and a thick carpet that looked as if you would sink into it.

A slight movement to her left caught her attention and she turned slowly—very slowly, damnable head—to see what it was. An ample face with a huge smile full of crooked teeth greeted her up close.

"It's so good to see yer Ladyship awake. We were so afeared for ye, we was!" the woman said brightly, fortunately keeping her voice low. Considering her size, it would have been natural for her to carry a loud voice. "Lizzie's gone to fetch 'is Lordship and let 'im know that yer back among us."

"May... may I have some water?" she heard a weak voice say. It felt like it was coming from her throat, but she wasn't sure.

"Of course, yer Ladyship, Bessie will take right care 'o you," she beamed, hurrying to pour water from a glass pitcher beside the bed.

The damnable pain was still running riot, so she reached up to touch the spot that hurt so terribly. She found a cloth barrier between her and the source.

"Oh, no, milady. You don't wanna be touchin' that. The doc says to leave it alone. Ye either get better or yer won't. They don't know much when it comes to those 'ead things, if ya ask me." The woman named Bessie slipped a strong, plump arm under her shoulders and lifted her easily as she brought the glass to her lips. She drank greedily. "Take yer time, milady, ye don't wanna drown the moment yer safe," teased Bessie good naturedly.

"Bessie?"

"Yes, mum?" Bessie replied, looking at her expectantly.

"Who am I?" The words seemed to echo around the room as Bessie froze solid as a stone. She hastily recovered herself before lowering the woman back into the pillows. She set the glass of water on the bedside table.

"Ye 'ad a bit of an accident. We ain't quite sure, but either yer 'orse threw yer Ladyship or you was knocked off by a tree branch." She settled gently on the bed despite her size as her voice became almost a cooing sound. "Yer in your 'ome. In yer own bed. Yer Grace would be Lady Katherine Eddington."

"Katherine? Katherine," she tried it out. "That doesn't sound right."

Just then the chamber door opened, and Lizzie hurried in, tossing a look over her shoulder at someone following. Bessie rose from the bed. Next to Bessie, Lizzie was a skinny pole with long, gangly arms. Her yellow hair stretched down her back in one long braid that had escaped her cap and she had an upturned nose that highlighted the innocence revealed by her freckled face.

A rotund, dark-suited man ambled in behind Lizzie. He was putting on spectacles and opening a small black case. He busily looked into her eyes and put his ear to her chest before holding her wrist. It was then she remembered that Bessie had mentioned His Lordship. Well, this certainly wasn't him. This was a doctor, she reasoned.

Suddenly, the room seemed to change. Katherine felt his presence before she saw him. He felt big and dark and imposing. She turned her aching head slightly and he stepped into her view, although he seemed to be standing away from the bed.

He was the most handsome man she had ever seen. His hands were behind him, his feet planted wide apart as if he were bracing for an attack. His long black hair had been tied carelessly back in a queue, allowing a few locks to escape, giving him a wild appearance. His full, sensuous lips were curled into a slight scowl. He had money to be sure, she could tell by his black velvet waistcoat and blizzard white cravat. His black breeches hugged his body, revealing its perfection, well-turned and finished off by black leather knee-high Hessian boots.

Her eyes couldn't help sliding slowly up and down what she guessed was a six-foot-two frame, from his broad shoulders which filled the room, or at least her vision of it, to his narrow waist set into solid hips and strong legs that testified to the fact that this male spent a lot of time riding horses.

The light shifted through the window and his beautiful blue eyes glittered, arresting her attention. She realized then that the room wasn't so much dark as his face was tan—and that, along with the white cravat, set his eyes apart from all else.

He shifted as if he were unaccustomed to her perusal or was made uneasy by it. At last, he spoke, but he still did not come near the bed.

"I see you are alive, Madame." His deep baritone voice almost sounded disappointed.

"Who are you?" she asked in that voice that was still strange to her ears. It sounded deep, almost husky. Wasn't it supposed to be lighter? Crisper?

Her question startled him, but he covered it quickly. Bessie stepped forward and his attention swung to her.

"Beggin' yer pardon, yer Lordship, but her Grace doesn't remember—much."

"Indeed?" his dark eyebrows went up in an attempt to hide his amusement.

"Not all together a surprise," replied the rotund man. "I thought just a thing might be possible." He leaned in closer to the tall, handsome man and whispered, but Katherine still heard him. "Tell her who you are but do try and be gentle. Go slow."

It was then the dark-haired man stepped closer to the bed, but no sign of amusement lingered. "I am

Lord Charles Eddington, sixth duke of Wescott. Your husband."

"That's impossible," she intoned as she closed her eyes against the pain she was still struggling with. "I'm not that lucky."

Had her eyes been open, she would have seen the startled shudder that passed uncontrollably through him. He studied her for several long moments, shifting with his agitation. Her eyes remained closed.

"Obviously, Madame needs her rest," he said finally and left the room. The doctor, Bessie and Lizzie stared after him.

The doctor cleared his throat before saying; "Yes, well..." before following the duke out. Katherine was sleeping and didn't hear the duke's words, but she felt him leave all the same and it roused her. She was thirsty again.

"Water please?" she managed.

Lizzie rushed forward to help but tripped over her feet, her hand knocking the water glass from the side table. It spilled on the side of the bed covers and onto the luscious carpet. Lizzie recoiled in absolute terror. Bessie grabbed her shoulders from behind to steady her and they held their breath. Katherine realized that they were waiting for her to react. They looked like they were being stared down by a wild animal.

"What is wrong? It was just an accident," she assured them, but they didn't move. Katherine forced herself into a sitting position by slowly swinging her legs out from under the covers and off the side of the bed. Her head swam.

"Milady, you shouldn't get up," Bessie pleaded, but didn't move.

"Someone has to, you both seemed to have lost your power of mobility."

With that, both began to move at once; Bessie urging her mistress back into bed and Lizzie sopping up the spill with a towel. Lizzie looked as if she were relieved that no retribution for her clumsiness was forthcoming, but she still kept a wary eye on Lady Eddington.

"I am sorry, my Lord, but the human brain is unpredictable," Doctor Williamson was intoning as the duke wore a path in the thick carpet of his library. Charles had brought the doctor with him from London when word of his wife's accident had reached him. "She may suddenly remember everything or then she may never again remember the past. If providence is with us, she will slowly retrieve her memory. But if it all comes tumbling back at a pace she is not ready for, well then..." His trailing sentence brought the duke up short.

"Are you saying it could kill her? Or that she would go insane?"

"Either could be a possibility, I should think," the doctor finished with a nod.

The duke's mouth curled into a slight smile as he turned away from the doctor so the old man wouldn't observe him. Death or insanity. He found himself thinking either would be an acceptable solution. If she went insane, he could petition for a divorce and be rid of her for good. If she died, well then... who needed a divorce?

"Well, if you will excuse me, your Grace, I'm for bed. I'll need an early start in the morning."

"You're leaving?" frowned the duke.

"Why, yes. She is well on her way to recovery—health-wise. There is no more that I can do for her. She needs her rest. The return of her memory is the job of Providence, not mine."

CHAPTER TWO

Sometime later, Katherine couldn't be sure how long, for she had dropped in and out of sleep, she felt a slight tremor. Forcing open her heavy lids, she focused on the foot of the bed. A small dark head was barely concealed by the heavily carved footboard. Since she wasn't going anywhere, Katherine patiently waited for the head to make the next move. After a while, a pair of dark eyes peeped over the footboard at Katherine.

"Who are you?" she asked quietly.

"Charles," replied the beautiful little boy as he stepped around the footboard, but he too, didn't move too close. Katherine estimated him to be around six, maybe seven. He was an exact replica of the duke.

"Come closer. Don't be afraid," she tried to smile encouragingly. He contemplated her for a moment before inching closer. She tapped her hand on the bed beside her. "Closer please. My head hurts so much that it's hard to look so far across the room."

The boy eyed her carefully. She could tell he was warring within himself. Why was he hesitating? she wondered.

"I can hardly move and you're obviously so much stronger than I, what do you have to fear?" she baited him.

He then hopped up a lot quicker than she thought he would. On closer inspection, she knew without a doubt that he was the duke's offspring and a future lady killer. She hoped not in the literal sense.

"Why are you hiding at the foot of the bed?"

"Papa said I was not to disturb you. He said you were playing a game. What game are you playing? Can I play mamma - er - your Grace?" He swallowed with difficulty, his eyes darting about in case he needed an escape route.

Mamma? She was a mother? She couldn't remember and yet...

She reached to tousle his hair and he jerked back, his arm going up to shield himself. Her hand froze. When he saw that he wasn't going to be hit, he slowly lowered his arm and sat upright. She carefully moved her fingers into his hair and began stroking him.

Here she was, laying in a bed in a room she had never seen before. Married to a man who obviously hated her and, hardest of all, the mother of a child who seemed to be afraid of her.

"I'm not playing a game. I honestly cannot remember this house, your father or—I'm afraid—you."

"Is it because of your bandage?" he asked, his eyes fixed on her forehead. She smiled as she reached up to touch the wrapping.

"Actually, it is what's under the bandage, young Charles. Have you ever hurt your head before?"

"Yes," he nodded vigorously as he lifted a dark lock off his brow. "My pony threw me the first time I rode him. But I could remember everything when I brushed myself off. 'Specially how mad at him I was!"

Katherine chuckled at his passionate response and was rewarded with a resonating shock of pain. She grimaced.

"Did I hurt you, your Grace?" he asked fearfully.

"No. No, sweetheart," she smiled through the pain as she gently stroked his back. "Can I ask a favor young Charles?"

"Of course, your Grace," he replied solemnly.

"Will you aid me in learning about my life before the accident?"

"Yes, your Grace. I will make it my duty," he straightened nobly.

"Thank you. Your help and your patience will be greatly appreciated." Her hand was now gently rubbing his shoulder and he suddenly threw his arms around her for a quick hug before launching himself from the bed. He stopped at the door, turned toward her and bowed respectfully before leaving.

She couldn't explain why, but Katherine suddenly burst into tears. She covered her mouth trying to keep the sobs from escaping and her shoulders heaved with the effort. She turned carefully so that she could bury her face in a pillow. She cried until she was asleep, her sobs mere hiccups that slowly faded.

The duke moved out of the shadowed doorway and stood beside the bed looking down at her. His hands were in tight fists at his side, his face like stone except for the pulse in his jaw. He had no idea what to make of her scene with his son or the unexpected show of tears. He had only seen his wife cry once in their entire married life. He had seen her temper, she had shouted and screamed, but never a tear save for that one night so long ago. To this day he still didn't know why she had cried. But that was the last moment of tenderness he had ever known from her. Maybe the injury had knocked some sense into her? But who knew if it would last?

Or maybe it was just the calm before the storm.

Scowling, the duke made his way downstairs and into his library. Old Maddy was there pouring a brandy, anticipating his master's need.

"How fair's her Grace, milord?" asked the butler. Maddy had been a family retainer for some fifty years, since he was a boy not much older than the duke's son. The duke tossed down the brandy and handed the empty glass back before going to the fireplace and glaring into the flames.

"She is up to something; I'd wager my fortune on it!" he declared as he shoved a large hand against the mantel piece to lean against. Maddy handed him another Brandy.

"To what purpose, milord?"

"Who knows? Her own amusement, no doubt," the duke grumbled, this time sipping his brandy. "She's played elaborate games before." Suddenly remembering, his head came up. "Any word regarding Sabrina yet?"

"No word, your Grace," Maddy replied gravely.

The duke stood straight and balled his left fist, resting it at the small of his back as he continued sipping his brandy. It was all very strange, he mused. A sudden thought struck him, causing him to smile.

"Do share, your Lordship. An old man could use a good smile," Maddy coaxed.

"Perhaps Sabrina was the cause of your mistress's head injury and left so she would not be punished for it. We all know the Duchess would have deserved it."

Maddy had the discipline and good grace not to smile. But he did mask his emotions by lowering his head.

"Ah, come Maddy. You know I speak the truth. There have been many a time when I've relished the idea of tightening my fingers around her slender white throat. Admit it, so have you."

"As you say, sir," replied Maddy in a neutral tone as the duke handed over the empty glass again, but this time he put up his hand to indicate he was through.

"The worse thing I ever did was marry that bitch and bring her into this house. I will always rue the day."

"But then, your Grace, you would not have your son and you know how deeply you love the lad," Maddy reasoned.

"Aye, that I do, Maddy. The duke's face and tone softened. That I do."

CHAPTER THREE

The sun was hidden behind the heavy curtains, but Katherine awoke just moments before Bessie entered with her breakfast tray.

"Mornin' your Grace," she smiled her big smile as she set the tray on the side table so she could throw open the draperies and arrange pillows around the Duchess. Katherine looked at the meager offerings on the tray.

"Is that doctor's orders?" she asked, cocking an eyebrow, but not without effort.

"No, Mum. Dry toast and tea. It's what you always order."

"What are they having downstairs?"

"Cook's made-up ham slices, kidneys, porridge, eggs and sweet tarts, Mum."

"I'll have one of each," sighed Katherine as her mouth watered and her stomach rumbled. Bessie looked at her dumbly. The two women stared at one another. "Have I grown an extra nose overnight?" asked Katherine as she felt her face.

"No, yer Grace. I'll bring another tray," Bessie replied in a small voice, the shock still residing in her face.

A huge sigh escaped Katherine as she turned her head toward the window. She wanted to rise and look out, curious about the grounds of what she was sure would be an estate, but any attempt to rise up made her head spin. Forced to remain still, she could only contemplate everyone's reaction to her.

There was fear and uncertainty in Bessie and Lizzie. Fear and longing in young Charles. And utter contempt from the duke. What manner of woman had she been before the accident that would illicit such reactions? Considering the water incident and young Charles knee-jerk reaction, she had to have been more than a mere shrew. Had she actually hit that sweet boy? Struck the servants? And what of the duke? He was a mountain. As hard as a rock. Surely, she had never attempted to pummel him?

She was sleeping again by the time Bessie returned with the new tray, but the wonderful breakfast smells quickly brought her around. Bessie could barely get a napkin under her chin before Katherine attacked the food as if she hadn't eaten in years. Bessie's mouth routinely fell open in amused gasps as she watched her mistress devour the meal. Her eyes were shining as she kept her Grace's teacup filled and dabbed a napkin at Katherine's chin occasionally.

The change in her Ladyship is so welcome, Bessie thought to herself. She wondered if the tantrums and tirades were now to be a thing of the past. Wondered if the servants would no longer have to use their serving trays as shields against flying objects her Grace was known for hurling over the smallest infractions.

"What?" Katherine queried; her mouth filled with the last morsel of ham in a completely unladylike manner. "You look about to cry."

"Tis nothing but 'appiness, I assure ye," smiled Bessie, unshed tears glittering in her eyes. "More tea, yer Grace?"

Eddington rode his dark stallion as if the devil herself was chasing him down. They flew over every bush and impediment in their pathway. Deacon snorted with delight at the challenges his master was guiding him through. The beast under him could not know the personal torment that his master was reliving in his head. His grim look etched deeply into his face as he reviewed all that had happened since the Duchess had been found lying injured in the woods, almost dead, only to awaken from her week-long coma.

Guilt. Ah, what a fine emotion. It riddled him mercilessly. He had wanted her to die, but damn her, she hadn't. It was shameful to want such a thing for your spouse. But he was bound to the cruel witch for the rest of his life, how could he be blamed for wanting to be free? He suddenly remembered the solid horseflesh beneath him and pulled Deacon to a slow trot. He patted his neck and smiled lovingly at the creature. He allowed Deacon to slow to a walk.

Charles thought about the Duchess' accident and the disappearance of her chambermaid Sabrina. It was a tight little mystery, but all that was eclipsed by the new personality his wife was insisting on projecting. He thought of the way her eyes had inspected him when she had first awakened. Not with the disdain she had shown since their wedding night, but with an intimate, raw appreciation. His belly tensed and he felt himself grow hard just as he had then. He had thought that since that horrible night so long ago, nothing she could say or do would ever unnerve him again. But he was wrong. Not only had she done it with a look, but upon hearing the announcement that he was her husband she had replied, I'm not that lucky.

Charles realized that he hadn't wanted the doctor to leave, not because he was concerned for his wife's welfare, but because that would mean he'd have to be alone with her. Alone? He had almost a hundred servants and his son in the house, certainly that did not qualify as being alone. He was feeling awkward. Awkward in his own house. He was spending more and more time away, keeping distance between himself and the she-devil he had married. If it weren't for his son, he thought he might never return home. No, that wasn't true either. He'd be damned if he let that bitch keep him from his own home. That was why he'd come back again and again. Yet, he was living in a townhouse in London while she had the run of his entire estate. Now that his son was older, he was taking young Charles to London with him. He knew that Charles was old enough and intelligent enough to realize that his mother didn't love him. That thought caused the duke actual physical pain. His thoughts drifted to last night and Katherine actually stroking her son.

"She's up to something," he cursed out loud.

I'm not that lucky, the words echoed through his brain. He hadn't slept at all that night. Merely paced the length of his chamber and back again until just before dawn when it had all become too much for him and he had sought out his favorite companion, Deacon. The great horse's head carried smartly to one side as the beast stepped up to a canter as soon as he hit the road toward his master's estate.

I'm not that lucky, the words made the rounds through his head again as he leapt down from Deacon and threw the reigns to his stable master, Gelroy. No, he would not think of her. He would not go to her room.

"Feed and water him well, treat him like the prince he is, for he has served me well this morning," proclaimed the duke as he patted the great horse's neck.

"Aye, your Grace. Come Deacon," clucked Gelroy with the same affection that the duke held for the beast. Gelroy was a stocky man, older than the duke, with long muscled hairy arms. He too had been with the family for as long as Charles could remember.

I'm not that lucky, echoed through him again. No. He would not go. The duke pulled off his riding gloves as he made his way inside. Maddy was there to receive them along with the duke's overcoat. He watched the duke's face as he looked up the great stairs toward her side of the house.

"The young master awaits you in the breakfast room, your Grace," Maddy offered.

"Yes, of course," replied the duke as his eyes remained on the staircase. Maddy moved off and, after a few moments, so did the duke.

Bessie's tread on the stairs attracted the duke's attention as he walked toward the breakfast room. He stopped and waited for her.

"Good mornin', yer Grace," smiled Bessie widely as she held up the tray with the empty dishes for his inspection. "Ate a whole tray, she did!"

"A whole tray?" he queried with a cocked black brow.

"Aye, sir. Maybe that blow made more than one improvement," she offered. The duke smiled as Bessie waddled off toward the kitchen. Bessie was a Godsend, he thought to himself. With Sabrina disappearing, no other servant was brave enough, or—he knew—possessed the desire, to attend the Duchess. But Bessie would face down a platoon of Dragoons for the duke. He looked up the stairs again.

CHAPTER FOUR

She was asleep. He stood over her and contemplated her face. How long had it been since he had seen it so serene? Unlined by fierce hatred and disdain for him and everything around him? He allowed his look to wander down her forehead, passed her closed lids and rest momentarily on her nose. He had never noticed it's beauty before. Had he ever really looked at it?

Her beauty reminded him of the day he had returned fresh from Cambridge and his father told him of his betrothal to Katherine. How beautiful she had looked, sitting in the garden reading her book. Looking back now, he realized that her acceptance to marry him had all been some sort of a ruse. But she was so damned beautiful, and she had let him kiss her that day in the garden. Intimately kiss her.

The duke unconsciously licked his lips as he looked down at his wife's sleeping form. His eyes fell to the rhythmic rise and fall of her full breasts covered by her gown. Breasts he hadn't seen or touched since before their son was born and then barely for she would not allow him to completely remove her night shift and insisted on all the candles being snuffed out.

That memory immediately plunged him into all the other memories from that first month together and his mouth hardened. He drew himself up straight and closed off his emotions less they slay him where he stood. He turned and strode toward the door.

"Your Grace?" her voice intoned quietly. He whirled around at the sound.

Katherine was startled to see such hatred in his eyes. How long had he been there? Had he been staring at her? And what could she have possibly done to deserve such a look? From her position in the bed, his loins were included within her field of vision without having to move her eyes and she noted the large bulge. Well, at least his hatred isn't one of indifference, she thought to herself. The duke composed himself quickly, his face taking on a neutral expression.

"How do you fair this morning?" he asked emotionless, as if he were meeting a mere acquaintance on the street.

"Better, thank you."

"Good," he said and turned on his heel, leaving her staring after him.

—Continued—

Don't miss out!

Visit the website below and you can sign up to receive emails whenever Jordan Rivers publishes a new book. There's no charge and no obligation.

https://books2read.com/r/B-A-YHHHB-KQPBD

BOOKS 2 READ

Connecting independent readers to independent writers.

Also by Jordan Rivers

Hunky Nerd Series
Hunky Nerd 1 & 2

Standalone
A Duchess's Redemption
Víspera de brujas
Witches' Eve
The Five Suitors
Empowered Survival: A Comprehensive Guide For Women
The Weekend Fisherman's Cookbook
Easy Fitness for Seniors
High Desert
How to Train for the Combine
Alto Desierto
Supervivencia Empoderada: ung guia completa para mujeres

About the Author

I started writing for fun when I was a kid but I didn't get serious about publishing until my 20s. After taking film and broadcasting in college I felt I'd found my true calling. I now write, direct, and produce ultra-low-budget movies. I've won two awards for my scripts; editor's choice for poetry and I'm published in paperback as well on Amazon. My first non-fiction book entitled, "I Know How You Feel..." is about my ten-year struggle with the death of my oldest son and how writing about it brought me back.

www.ingramcontent.com/pod-product-compliance
Lightning Source LLC
Chambersburg PA
CBHW021233130726
47988CB00002B/952